This Isn't About Eating Cat Food and Working Harder.

It's about getting out of debt once and for all. It's about you getting out of debt—no matter how long you've been there or how much you owe.

It's Not About Clipping Coupons or Saving String.
It's Not a Get-Rich Scheme or an Investment System.

It's a clear and simple program that will enable you to free yourself from debt and to stay free forever.

Be as skeptical as you want. But if you follow this program, you'll still get out of debt. These are not simply theoretical ideas. They've been tested and proven over the last ten years by thousands of men and women who have already used them to free themselves from debt and thousands more are using them right now to do the same thing. You can too.

This program works. It's that simple.

How to Get Out of Debt, Stay Out of Debt & Live Prosperously*

*(Based on the Proven
Principles and Techniques
of Debtors Anonymous)*

Jerrold Mundis

Bantam Books

HOW TO GET OUT OF DEBT,

STAY OUT OF DEBT

& LIVE PROSPEROUSLY

PUBLISHING HISTORY
Bantam hardcover edition / February 1988
Bantam paperback edition / April 1990
Bantam revised trade paperback edition / January 2003

Book design by Sabrina Bowers

Library of Congress Cataloging-in-Publication Data
Mundis, Jerrold J.
How to get out of debt, stay out of debt & live prosperously/Jerrold Mundis.—Bantam
rev. trade pbk. ed.
p.   cm.
"Based on the proven principles and techniques of Debtors Anonymous."
ISBN 0-553-38202-0
1. Finance, Personal.   2. Debt.   I. Debtors Anonymous.   II. Title.
HG179.M855   2003
332.024'02—dc21   2002074739
Published simultaneously in the United States and Canada

PRINTED IN THE UNITED STATES OF AMERICA

RRH 10 9 8 7 6 5 4 3 2 1

*This, with gratitude, is for John
and for my sons Shep and Jesse
and for Suzanne*

CONTENTS

How to Get Out of Debt, Stay Out of Debt & Live Prosperously

PREFACE

This is a book about debt and about freeing yourself from debt—forever.

You, like me, like every other American, are either:

1. Overwhelmed by your debts
2. Sometimes uneasy about them and worried that you might be getting in too deep
3. Or you have a surplus of money and rarely think about debt or credit at all

Most of us fall into the first or second of these groups. If *you* do, then this book is for you. It will teach you, step by step, how to liberate yourself from debt, stay free of it forever, and live a life of prosperity and abundance from then on. Even if issues of debt and credit are largely irrelevant to you, you'll still find valuable material here that will help you manage your money more effectively, bring more of it in, and use it in more pleasurable ways.

I first wrote this book in 1986, at the end of my own long spiral downward into debt and into the pain and even despair that inevitably accompany it. The power of the concepts and techniques I presented here for stopping that terrible decline, getting free of debt, and learning how to live prosperously has been proved repeatedly since then by the hundreds of thousands of men and women who have used them to do just that and who are using them to do so today. For many, these concepts and techniques have become a way of life, as they have for me.

This new edition of *How to Get Out of Debt, Stay Out of Debt & Live Prosperously* retains all the essential material of the original. I have revised it to reflect changes in society, to update numbers because of inflation, to expand some material, and to add an entirely new chapter, called "Couples and Families." If there was anything I would have done differently when I first wrote the book, I decided in later years, it would have been to include counsel specifically for people who were part of a couple or family or were raising children alone, to help them practice the rest of the program more easily. So what I have done is adapted a chapter from one of my later books, *Earn What You Deserve: How to Stop Underearning & Start Thriving*, where I did address those circumstances for use here in this new edition.

If you are new to *How to Get Out of Debt, Stay Out of Debt & Live Prosperously*, I promise you that you'll find the same freedom and joy in it that I and so many others have and continue to find. If you are revisiting the book here in this new edition, I promise you that you will find in it renewed enthusiasm for this way of life and powerful reinforcement for living it. Either way, Godspeed.

This Isn't About Eating Cat Food and Working Harder

It's about getting out of debt once and for all. It's about *you* getting out of debt—no matter how long you've been there or how much you owe.

It's not about clipping coupons or saving string. It's not a get-rich scheme or an investment system.

It's Back to the Black, a clear and simple program that will enable you to free yourself from debt, to stay free forever, and to bring prosperity into your life.

Sure. Uh-huh.

Be as skeptical as you want. But if you follow this program, you'll still get out of debt. These are not simply theoretical ideas. They've been tested and proven over the last fifteen years by *hundreds of thousands* of men and women who have already used them to free themselves from debt;

many thousands more are using them right now to do the same thing. You can too.

This program works. It's that simple.

You Are Not Alone

Discussion of personal finance, particularly indebtedness, may be the last American taboo. Most of us shrink from it as we would from something obscene. Yet personal debt is epidemic in America: More than thirty million Americans are overwhelmed by it at this very moment, many only a paycheck or two ahead of catastrophe, and millions more are living in daily stress and discomfort because of it.

In 1988, when this book was first published, personal bankruptcy stood at 600,000 cases per year; fifteen years later, it stands at 1,200,000 per year. Consumer debt was $700 billion then; now it is $1,600 billion. Personal income grew at five percent a year. Personal debt by half again as much.

Trouble with debt cuts across all social strata—from doctors and lawyers to carpenters and teachers, from psychologists and executives to house painters and firemen, from consultants and secretaries to stock clerks and stockbrokers.

You are not alone in this.

Some of us are earning well over $100,000 or $200,000 a year, others are on unemployment. Some owe tens and even hundreds of thousands of dollars, others no more than $1,000 or $5,000. But debt is debt, no matter how much we earn or how much we owe. And sooner or later it can, and frequently does, poison our lives.

What Debt Does to Us

Eventually, we begin to juggle our money week to week and month to month, trying to stay on top of bills and responsibilities. We walk a tightrope and live in apprehension of impending disaster, in fear that we're going to run out, that we won't have enough, that we'll be caught in a squeeze, that we'll be hauled into court.

This fear exerts ever more pressure on us. It begins to disrupt our lives and personal relationships. It sucks the joy and pleasure out of our days. The emotional and physical toll becomes enormous. In time, it exhausts us. We come to feel defeated and hopeless. We grow depressed. We live in anxiety and despair. We experience pain and perhaps even impulses toward suicide.

Being in debt, regardless of the level of discomfort, is an unpleasant condition for anyone. It is also wholly unnecessary.

Where This Program Comes From

Debtors Anonymous is a self-help organization that was founded in 1976. It has grown rapidly since then and now has chapters across the United States and in several foreign countries as well. The only requirement for membership is a desire to stop incurring debt. It is wholly self-supporting through the voluntary contributions of its members, whose primary purpose is to remain solvent and to help other people in debt achieve solvency.

Many of the concepts, techniques, and strategies in the Back to the Black program originated in Debtors Anonymous (DA), though this book is in no way connected with that organization, which as a policy neither supports nor opposes any outside projects. Other material in the program comes from individual members of DA and via complementary sources such as consciousness seminars, metaphysical disciplines, and prosperity workshops.

In the end, all this material has been filtered through my own personal experience and evolves from my close contact

and work with literally hundreds of men and women—
and by extension, thousands more—who have successfully
worked these principles and freed themselves from debt.

Each has his or her own unique story.

In my case, I was $50,000 in debt when I began to practice
this program back in 1984 (the equivalent of $85,000 today),
had expenses of $3,000 per month, and had a guaranteed in-
come of only $350 per month, from a small mortgage on a
piece of property I'd once owned. How I'd gotten into that
position was, I thought, due to several circumstances: the erratic nature of a freelance writer's income, a divorce, an illness, and changes in the publishing industry that resulted in
a couple of career setbacks. That's what I thought then. I
think differently now—because of what I've learned, which
became the material for this book.

From the day I committed to this program, I never borrowed another dime. And since then I have liquidated my
debt, steadily escalated my income, dramatically improved
the quality of my life in such areas as vacations, entertainment, wardrobe, and possessions, and, most importantly,
have won a growing psychological and emotional freedom
from the stress and pain of debt.

So has Paul, a forty-year-old Chicago real estate salesman.
Paul was down $58,000 and on the verge of bankruptcy
when he began this program. In five years, he repaid his
creditors in full and increased his income from $65,000 to
$90,000.

Christine, a thirty-four-year-old commercial illustrator
who lives in Boston, owed $19,000. Today, six years later, she
owes nothing. And her income jumped from $30,000 to
$75,000.

Vivian, who is in her seventies, still works in high fashion
in New York, though not as many hours as she did when I
first wrote about her a decade and a half ago. Vivian is also
free of debt now, and has been for several years, even though
she began her recovery owing $240,000.

Tony is still moving toward freedom. Twenty-seven, Tony is a painter in the Southwest who also works as a carpenter. A year and a half ago, he owed $18,000. Today he owes less than $15,000. Equally important to him, he can now spend significantly more time on his painting than he had been able to before.

There are countless more.

With this program, if you choose, you too can do what they have done.

You Don't Have to Go One More Dollar into Debt

Sure I don't. And if I clap very hard and believe, Tinkerbell will live.

But it's true—*hundreds of thousands* have stopped, and have liberated themselves completely from debt using the principles and techniques in this book, sometimes from spectacular amounts.

You will too.

Begin reading, and know that you've just taken the first step toward freeing yourself from debt now and forever.

PART I

THE
DEBT SPIRAL

1

WHAT IS DEBT?

I.O.U.

In its simplest definition, you are in debt when you owe some person or institution money. We need a refinement though. For our purposes, a secured loan is *not* a debt, even though money has been loaned to you.

The Secured Loan

To secure something is to make it safe. When you secure a loan, you free the lender from any risk of losing his money. That's why he's willing to lend it to you—he has no fear of loss.

Your word, your good faith, even your unfailing history of repayment do not secure a loan. What happens if you have medical emergencies, lose your job, or simply go bonkers and run off to Brazil—if, for *any* reason, you just don't have the money to pay the loan back? The lender loses his money, that's what.

Collateral, in its primary definition, is something that runs side by side with something else. In financial terms, collateral is property you pledge to the lender or actually give to him to hold during the course of the loan. That property is security, it's what makes the lender's money safe or secured. When you pay him back, he returns it to you.

A loan from a pawnshop is a classic example. You bring your camera to the pawnbroker. He loans you $75. When you repay him the $75 (plus interest, of course), he gives your camera back to you. If you don't repay him, he keeps your camera. You don't own your camera anymore, but you don't owe him $75 either. The loan is over.

Fine, you say, but *you're* not interested in hockshops and cameras. You're talking *big* money—$5,000, $50,000, more.

The Numbers Don't Make Any Difference.

A loan is a loan, whether it's for $5, $500, or $50,000. And collateral is collateral, whether it's a television set or a television station.

One of the most common forms of secured loan is a mortgage. Let's say I'm buying a house for $150,000. I've saved $30,000, which I use for the down payment. The bank likes my job history, my salary, and my credit record. They have confidence in me. But that confidence alone isn't enough to persuade them to lend me the additional $120,000 I need, not without strings attached. Life's too unpredictable for that. So they require me to give them a mortgage on my house—a document that generally grants them all legal rights to it if I default, that is, if I fail to make my loan payments for a specified period of time, usually about four months. The bank then has the right to foreclose the mortgage, to take possession of my house in lieu of what I owe them, sell it, and keep the proceeds or the bulk of the proceeds for themselves, thus recouping their $120,000. I've secured the loan by pledging my house as collateral. I've eliminated the risk that the bank will lose their money if they lend it to me.

Car loans work the same way. I buy a new Chevy for $24,000. I put $5,000 of my own money down and borrow the balance, $19,000, from a bank or from General Motors. To get the financing, I sign a document that gives the lender all rights and title to the car if I don't pay the loan back.

If I default in either of these cases, I lose my house or my car. That would be painful, but I would not owe money to anyone. I would not go into debt—*provided* I had made a large enough down payment. That is an important provision. Normally what happens in the case of a house or a car walked away from, foreclosed upon, repossessed or otherwise reclaimed by the lender, is that the lender sells off the property, deducts the amount received from the outstanding balance, and arrives at a new balance owed: the old one minus the proceeds of the sale.

Let's say that Frank, who still owes $9,000 on his Honda, is moving to another state and a new job where, among other benefits, he will have the use of a car. He's broke and under time pressure. So he turns the car over to the creditor (almost always a bank), and says, "Here, it's all yours. The loan is over." But it's not. The bank now has Frank's car, the collateral for the loan, but the loan is still in effect. The bank, which is a business, not a social welfare agency, wants to clear this loan quickly and with minimal effort. So it wholesales the Honda out, getting $5,000 for it. Frank still owes the creditor $4,000 on the loan and has all the legal obligations and liabilities that any debtor does. He is still as vulnerable to the creditor if he defaults as he is to any other creditor.

The same scenario is true with a house. But there the bank will usually have required a large enough down payment so that the house can be turned over for the amount still owed, unless there has been a major decline in the real estate market.

The key, then, in these situations, is to put enough money down on a car or house so that you have sufficient equity in it, should you need to liquidate it, that you can do so for at least the amount you still owe on it. Selling a car or house yourself and paying off the creditor is always better than turning it back to the creditor, even if the creditor could liquidate it for the balance you still owe. This is for reasons relating to your credit history, which we'll discuss in a later chapter.

A cash loan can also be secured. Of course the collateral has to be worth at least as much, and usually more, than the amount borrowed. No bank will accept $1,000 worth of stock certificates as collateral against a $5,000 loan, just as no pawnbroker will lend me $50 if I give him my Bic lighter to hold.

These are examples of collateral often used to secure cash loans:

- Bearer bonds
- Stock certificates
- Home equity, in the form of a second mortgage
- Parcels of land or other real estate
- Inventory
- Works of art
- Whole life insurance policies
- Precious metals
- An owned franchise
- Copyrights
- Patents
- A business

As anyone who's in debt knows very well, banks and financial institutions aren't the only places we can get a loan. We borrow from employers in the form of salary advances, from the government, from colleges and universities for educational loans, from business associates, from acquaintances and coworkers, from friends and relatives.

The most frequent loan in America is probably the one taken from a friend:

"Can you let me have $5 till tomorrow?"

"I need $20 till payday."

"Can you spare $300 till my commission check comes in?"

"My broker's check won't reach me for another week. Can you spot me $1,500 till then?"

The loan from family members is also common. Young couples setting up household or buying their first house frequently borrow from their families. I bought my own first house in 1971. Everything I'd saved went for the down payment and closing costs. There were several other expenses involved in moving my family from a city apartment to a house in the mountains, so I borrowed $7,500 from my father.

Houses, of course, aren't the only things for which we tap relatives. We borrow from them when we're between jobs, for education, vacations, Christmas buying, for furniture, medical expenses, big tax bills, births, marriages, divorces, to get over a hump, or when things are difficult in general.

These loans are usually given on good faith alone; but occasionally they're secured too. There's even more latitude in finding collateral for a personal loan than there is for a commercial loan. Commercial lenders want collateral for which there's a ready market and a constant demand, which assures them they can convert it to cash immediately if the borrower defaults. While friends or relatives might eventually prefer to do the same thing, they're usually satisfied with collateral in the form of something they'd like to own or use themselves, such as a video camera.

As collateral on a $2,500 loan, I once offered a friend an antique ivory statue he'd always admired. He didn't want collateral from me at all, but for my own reasons (which aren't relevant here, but will be later) I was determined that this loan be genuinely secured. He accepted my resolve, but still refused to remove the statue from my house. What we finally agreed on was this: I assigned to him through my literary agent—to become effective at his request—all income from one of my books up to the amount of $2,500. He's a novelist himself, and that assignment was satisfactory and pleasing to us both.

The possibilities for collateral on personal loans are nearly limitless. For example, you can use:

- Anything that could secure a commercial loan
- A VCR
- A piece of jewelry
- A fur coat
- A work of art
- A musical instrument
- An antique
- A computer
- A coin collection
- A set of encyclopedias
- A sewing machine
- Luggage
- Furniture
- A camera
- A snowmobile
- A power tool
- A rug

To sum it up, a secured loan is this: Someone lends you money, you give him an article of equivalent or greater value to hold until you pay him back.

Why Secured Loans Are Not Debt

From a strict point of view, a secured loan *is* debt: It's money you "owe." But there is a difference, and that difference is *crucial*.

If things go wrong, for any reason at all, and you can't repay the loan, what happens? You forfeit your property.

That may be painful, but *you are not obligated to pay money to anyone.*

You walk away clean. You don't owe anyone money. You're not in debt.

This Is It

Debt is:

1. Any amount of cash you borrow without putting up collateral
2. Any credit extended to you
3. Any service you take without paying for at the moment you receive it

Some common examples of incurring debt are:

- You're short this week, so you tap a friend at the office for $20.
- You need $500 to tide you over for a month, so you borrow it from your bank on your signature alone.
- You need a new winter coat but you don't have the money, so you call your parents and borrow it from them.
- You're out with a friend, you want to pick something up from a store, but you don't have enough cash, so you borrow a few dollars from her.
- You need your tax refund now and can't wait for it to arrive, so you ask your brother for $300.
- You buy a compact disc player from Macy's and charge it to your account.
- You gas up your car on your Mobil card.
- You go out to dinner and hand the waiter your Visa card.
- You fly to Chicago to spend Thanksgiving with your relatives and put the tickets on your American Airlines card.
- You buy your spring wardrobe on your Bloomingdale's card.

- You charge a new lawn mower to your Sears account.
- You need your car fixed but you can't pay your mechanic till next month; that's fine with him, so he does the work.
- Your child's college tuition is due, so you request an advance on salary or commissions.
- You need two caps and a root canal, but you don't have the money, so you arrange with your dentist to pay him off over the next several months.

These are all debts. You owe money to these people. They have no collateral from you: Your dentist can't sell the plaster cast of your mouth, Sears can't convert your signature into cash.

Take a few minutes for a discovery process here. On a pad of paper, write down any of the above, or variations on them, that you've done yourself over the past twelve months.

Draw a line beneath the list.

Now make a second list. Include here all the other ways you've incurred debt in the same period that aren't mentioned in the first list.

Now get creative. Make a third list, placing on this one all the ways you've heard through which your friends incur debt, then add every other way you can imagine.

Take a good look at these lists. They're a lot longer than you would have thought, aren't they? And they all add up to the same thing—debt.

This Is It Too

But we're not done yet. There are other, more subtle ways to incur debt.

What happens when you get behind on your rent?

.   .   .

My rent is $1,300 per month. Let's say it's July now. And let's say that last month I finally went for the eye exam I'd been putting off. It had been three years and my ophthalmologist wanted to do a full scan, which was sensible. My eyes proved healthy, but I did need a new prescription. The exam was $300, a new pair of glasses $225. My television, possibly in a gesture of sympathy with my old glasses, decided to commit suicide at the same time. So I bought a new one for $400. And, since I don't usually keep such things in mind, I was unhappily surprised to find that the premium for my life insurance was due, for $400. That's $1,325 I hadn't planned on spending in June.

Money's tight. So I don't pay my rent in July, planning to catch up in August. What I've done is taken a service—the use of my apartment—without paying for it.

I owe money; I've incurred a debt.

Could I have paid my rent? Sure. I might have arranged with my ophthalmologist to pay him off over a couple of months, bought my glasses on an American Express card, and put the television on Visa.

Either way, I go into debt.

Falling behind on unsecured obligations, then, is the second category of debt. The most common areas in which we do this are:

- Rent
- Telephone service
- Utilities (gas, electricity, water)
- Federal, state, and local income taxes
- Property taxes
- Alimony and child support
- Tuition
- Credit card bills (penalties for late or missed payments)
- Charge account statements (penalties for late or missed payments)
- Fuel bills

Turn to a fresh page on your pad of paper. Jot down the number of times you've been late by a month or more in any of these areas. Then add any more in which you were late that aren't included here. Now add any area you can think of where falling behind might be possible.

Surprising just how many ways there are to go into debt, isn't it? There's a whole supermarket of opportunities out there.

Debt, then, comes in almost limitless variations, but it's not hard to recognize once we're clear on what it is—borrowing cash without collateral, buying goods or taking services without paying for them immediately, and falling behind in unsecured obligations.

That recognition is a good start.

2

THE NATURE
OF DEBTING

"**D**ebt" is a noun. It has never been used as a verb—
"to debt." But we're going to coin it that way; it helps
us distinguish such use of money from other types of spending and from secured loans.

There are three kinds of debting: compulsive, problem-
atic, and reasonable.

Compulsive Debting

Throw out all the psychological jargon you've heard about
compulsion. Basically, a compulsion is simply an act that is
repeated over and over. It's motivated by an internal reason
or set of reasons, usually subconscious. Some compulsions
are harmless, such as arranging pens on a desk or cans on a
shelf in a certain order. Generally we think of them as no
more than habits or personal preference, if we think of
them at all.

When a compulsion is harmful—serious drinking or
overeating, for example—we try to deny that it's a compulsion. We manufacture excuses for it: "Hey, I work hard, and

I need a couple of drinks to unwind." We minimize the destructive consequences: "So I'm carrying a few pounds too much, it's no big deal, I'll knock 'em off by summer." We even claim that the consequences of our behavior are actually the cause of the behavior: "I do this because my life is pressured, hard, and painful"—when in fact life has become pressured, hard, and painful because of what we do.

Barbara, a divorced dental technician, insisted that she *had* to charge her son's new school clothes. He'd outgrown his old ones, and she didn't have the money to pay for the new ones. She was absolutely right. He *did* need new clothes, and she *didn't* have the money. But what she refused to see was *why* she didn't have the money—because most of her discretionary income had to be used for payments on her two credit cards, her department store account, and a personal bank loan, which were already costing her a total of $525 per month.

These were payments on debts Barbara had incurred over the previous year. Just a single month's worth—$525—would have been more than enough to buy her son's clothes. But the money wasn't available to her; she had to pay it to her creditors. So the pressure Barbara felt—her current need for money—was in fact the direct result of her previous debting. If she hadn't debted before, she would have had enough to meet her needs now. Like other compulsions, compulsive debting feeds on itself: the more you do it, the more problems that inevitably result; the more problems that result, the more you do it to obtain relief from these new problems.

Barbara bought $300 worth of clothes for her son, paying for them with a credit card. Her installment payment on that new debt, the clothes she charged, cost her another $23 per month. That raised the total of her monthly payments from $525 to $548. As a result, she now had even less discretionary income to spend each month on her normal expenses. Once again, her available money had diminished, making her life more pressured and difficult.

What happens when Barbara hits the next unexpected expense—an illness requiring a visit to the doctor, a car tire that has to be replaced, an appliance that wears out? She'll debt again, telling herself she simply *has* to. The total amount of her debt will increase again, her monthly payments will rise once more, and her life will become even harder, the pressure greater.

Compulsive debting means nothing more or less than that you repeatedly incur new debt despite the negative emotional and financial consequences that follow. Each time, you find a way to justify the new loan or late payment or use of credit, or turn to them in order to obtain relief from pressure you perceive as intolerable.

But it doesn't work. It only gets worse.

Problem Debting

The difference between problem debting and compulsive debting is largely one of frequency, scale, and intensity: A problem debtor doesn't debt as often as a compulsive debtor, or borrow as much, or experience financial trouble and emotional pain as severely as the compulsive debtor.

Yet.

Some people go into problem debting because of a temporary situation, such as a career difficulty, or because they don't realize at first just how steadily their debts are beginning to mount. Then either they're able to change the situation or they recognize they're getting in too deep and bring their debting to a halt.

But in many cases, if not most, problem debting is simply compulsive debting in the making. An overwhelming debt structure doesn't pop full-blown into our lives like

Athena from the head of Zeus. We build it slowly, piece by piece.

In my own case, it was seventeen years in the making.

Reasonable Debting

If you're free of any kind of problem with debt, it's reasonable to pay for dinner with a credit card. Or replace a failing washing machine and pay for the new one over the next twelve months. Or perhaps finance a vacation with a loan. Generally, this kind of debting occurs when you've been meeting heavy expenses recently—a child's tuition, major home repairs—and there's something you'd like or need now that would be inconvenient or difficult to pay for immediately; the stock market, for example, is in a downswing and you'd rather not liquidate assets at the moment, or perhaps you have money locked up in a certificate of deposit and can't redeem it for another month or two.

Sometimes life takes an unexpected turn. You lose your job, for example, and can't find another one for a few months. So you tighten up your lifestyle, live on your savings while you look for a new job, exhaust them, then borrow from your brother to keep going. You're hired, you pay your brother back over the next six months, then relax the austerities you imposed upon yourself and begin putting money into savings again. Or perhaps you don't make as much as you thought you would after you graduate from college. Your rent and student loan payments eat up a big chunk of your salary. For a year and a half your father sends a monthly check to help out. You finally get a promotion and a raise, and now begin to handle your expenses and obligations yourself.

In these situations, it's assumed that you have no significant history of debting, that you're not already carrying substantial debt, and that under ordinary circumstances you would not have a problem meeting your usual bills and expenses.

To determine whether or not your debting is reasonable, there's one very simple question to ask: Are your debts causing you any trouble, on any level at all?

If they are, your debting is probably not reasonable. The following chapter will help you eliminate any doubts you might have and help you determine just how serious a problem your debting may or may not be.

3

WARNING SIGNS

There are numerous warning signs along the road to debt, but they go mostly unnoticed until we're already in serious trouble—until we're unable to meet our bills, pressed by angry creditors, or threatened with legal action. If more than a few of these apply to you, or if any are routine in your life, then you have a debt problem or are likely to be on your way to one.

Is It the 15th Already?

This month's bills start coming in before you've cleared last month's. You meant to get to them, but you got caught up in other things. You're surprised to find that the phone bill is still there. Somehow you didn't get to the rent or send the dentist his check. You're frustrated when you begin to write the checks. There are more bills than you thought. It seems you're always behind.

- You know what past-due notices look like.
- Your bank has been informed that you haven't paid your property taxes yet.

- Your American Express bill shows a balance from last month and reminds you that payment in full is required upon receipt.
- The hardware store sends a letter telling you you're in arrears and requests that you send a check at once.

These rarely surprise you. You don't slap your forehead and say, "Oh my God, how could I have forgotten?" Uh-uh. You're familiar with this kind of communication, and your usual response is annoyance, depression, or frustration.

You've had to get on the phone and argue, apologize, or express your indignation because the telephone or utility company is going to cut off service unless payment is made immediately.

You've paid a certain bill only after receiving a threat from a creditor's legal department or a collection agency.

You resent your bills in general. You often say to yourself, "They just don't stop!" or "God, won't they ever leave me alone?"

The Unopened Mail

You avoid opening letters for fear of new bills or trouble with a creditor. The only mail you're truly comfortable with is from friends or relatives—unless you owe them money too. Bills and letters from creditors get put in an ever-increasing pile on a corner of your desk or dumped into a drawer.

Larry, a chain-store manager, used to put his into a shopping bag. He had two bags stuffed to capacity when he began this program—practically every bill and past-due notice he'd received in the previous year was packed into those bags. He was $46,000 in debt at that point.

This is the ostrich syndrome, sticking your head in the sand. As long as you don't have to see the bills, you can tell yourself they're not there. This syndrome can become so pervasive that any communication of a potentially financial nature becomes a threat. The possibility of a neutral or even beneficial contact never occurs to you.

Six months after she had stopped debting, Mona, a florist, was still so gripped by this fear that she panicked when a letter from the IRS arrived. She wouldn't open it for a week. Her anxiety mounted each day. When she finally did work up the courage, she found it contained a refund check for $270. Years of debting had left her nearly incapable of conceiving that an envelope from the IRS could contain anything but a demand for more money.

The Unbalanced Account

You rarely keep a running balance in your checkbook. You hardly ever reconcile your balance at the end of the month when you receive your statement. You tell yourself it's too much trouble. Or you simply don't want to see the bad news. Consequently, you never know how much you actually do have in the account. Somewhere around a thousand, you think, if you're willing to think about it at all. And that guess usually substantially overestimates the real amount.

The Unsent Check

This is a numbers game. You pretend you have more money than you really do. It was one of my own favorites. I *did* keep a running balance in my checkbook. But what I also did, and what other numbers players do, was delay writing checks until the last possible moment, until I was on the verge of incurring late charges, calls from creditors, or cancellation or shut-off notices. By hanging on to the money, I could look at my checkbook and see that I had a comfortable margin of around $2,000. Everything was okay, right? I had enough.

It was a con job. I didn't do it consciously, but I did it nonetheless. The sense of security it provided was false. If I'd paid those backlogged bills immediately, my balance of $2,000 would have dropped by $1,000; and looking at that, I would have been forced to confront the uncomfortable fact that $1,000 was all I had left with which to face $2,500 worth of expenses and incoming bills—that I was going to come up short for the month by $1,500.

The numbers player defends his balance fiercely. He resists mailing the checks until he absolutely has to. That imaginary balance is necessary, if he's to have any comfort or relief at all.

Not Much Down

At one time you paid cash or wrote a check for most of the things you bought, especially smaller items like a purse or a Walkman. But now you charge most of them to your credit card or store account.

When you purchased a large item such as a freezer or car, you used to make a sizeable down payment, keeping your monthly installments low. But you don't do that anymore. Your down payments have grown smaller and smaller, your installments larger. If you're offered a choice of time periods in which to pay, you'll take the longer period in order to reduce the monthly amount, two years instead of one, three instead of two.

You search for items offered at lowered down payments or on lengthened payment schedules. You consider yourself a smart shopper because of this. When you find one, you're pleased that it's within reach now.

The Department Stores

The total amount you've charged at any given store, or at several stores, has been rising steadily. Rarely do you ever reduce your balance to zero. It may come down for a while but all that means is that you have some maneuvering room. Soon there's something else you want or need, so you buy it, charging it, and the upward drift begins again.

Cash Advances

You use your credit card, or the overdraft privilege on your checking account, to obtain spending money or to pay a pressing bill while you're "stretching through."

A Couple of Bucks Till Tomorrow

You're frequently short by a few dollars. So you regularly borrow small amounts of cash from family, friends, and coworkers for a day or two.

It's the Adult Thing to Do

You associate charging and the use of credit with maturity and success. Your American Express card informs the world that you're someone to reckon with. You're proud of your top-of-the-line cards: your gold card, platinum card, premium card, preferred customer card. They don't give credit to losers, do they? You get a high when you whip out your card, a rush of good feeling when you tell a clerk to charge it.

An invitation to accept new credit pleases you—especially when the letter informs you that you've been selected for this privilege because you've proven yourself a person of worth, accomplishment, and responsibility. You're proud that you've been preapproved for credit and that all you have to do is sign your name and return the agreement.

You have a variety of credit cards—Visa, MasterCard, American Express, Mobil Oil, Carte Blanche, Diners Club, United Airlines, BF Goodrich, and others—and charge accounts at several local department stores. You're always interested when you hear about a new card and wonder if you have a need for this one too or might be able to put it to good use.

If One Is Good, Two Are Better

You have more than one Visa or MasterCard. You hold the extras in reserve, bringing a new one into play when you reach the maximum credit on the old one. A variation is to spread the total amount of your charging across three or four Visas or MasterCards issued to you by different banks.

I Handled That, by God

You have an inordinate sense of accomplishment over meeting routine financial responsibilities like rent and utility bills. You're proud of yourself for paying for the basics each month—food, shelter, and clothing. You feel you've done something impressive.

Money Is a Personal Matter

You find money an embarrassing or unfit subject for conversation. You're reluctant to participate in what should be a normal discussion about money. You view any mention of personal finances as a breach of etiquette, and you remove yourself from the situation if people begin to talk about it.

Even the *thought* of ever telling anyone how much you make or how much you owe makes your heart pound, your breath go shallow, and your palms start to sweat.

The Canceled Account

A bank has canceled your credit card or a store has canceled your charge account because of nonpayment or repeated late payments. You're either depressed or angry about this, and may claim that they treated you unfairly, that the fault is theirs.

Saved by the Bell

You frequently dig in and wait anxiously for the next money you expect—a paycheck, commission check, contract payment, or even a loan. You hold off paying bills, you tell friends and creditors you'll have the money shortly. And when the money does come, you experience a great sense of relief.

Who Knows What the Details Are?

You're largely ignorant of the terms of your various loans, credit card agreements, and charge accounts. You don't know how to read a statement, what the various figures on it mean, which ones tell you what portion of this month's payment goes toward the principal and what portion to the finance charge. You don't know what interest rate you're paying Visa, for example. You don't know how many months it will take you to pay off the jacket you charged at Marshall Field's. You don't have any idea what the difference is between simple and compound interest.

Usually, most of what you know about your credit arrangements is how much your top limit is.

Minimums

You rarely write a check against a charge account or credit card balance for anything more than the minimum payment due. Your balance generally hovers near the maximum. If it does fall, you charge something new and it shoots right back up again.

Next Month Is Next Month

You're not concerned about bills that don't have to be paid this month. So long as you can make this month's payments, everything is just fine.

You're caught off guard, you're annoyed and feel pressured when the calendar changes, and suddenly you realize this month you have to face property taxes, an insurance premium, a business trip, a birthday, or Christmas shopping, something you "knew" was approaching, but that somehow you didn't give much thought to and for which you're now unprepared.

You have little or no savings, investments, or assets. There's nothing for contingencies. One serious hit—losing your job, a fire, a medical emergency—would wipe you out. Month by month, practically every dollar you get in goes right back out.

Kite Flying

Circumstances sometimes force you to kite a check— write one for more money than you actually have in the bank. This takes different forms.

It's Thursday. Sheila gets paid every two weeks. Payday is tomorrow. She has $5 left in her checking account and just enough in her purse to make it home tonight. But she has to pick up a prescription from the drugstore, she needs something for breakfast, and she's going to a friend's home for dinner, which means, since it'll be late when the evening's over, that she'll want to take a cab home.

So she pays for her prescription with a check, stops at the supermarket, where she buys a few things and writes a check for $20 over the register, which gives her the added cash she needs. She figures she'll deposit her paycheck tomorrow afternoon, that these checks won't reach her bank until Monday, and that by then there'll be enough in her account to cover them.

Ray, on the other hand, has had a lot of unexpected expenses and hasn't paid his garage bill for a couple of months. He's told he has to or he can't park there anymore. Even though he won't have the money to cover it for a couple of weeks, he writes a check. He knows that by the time the check reaches the management company and is entered in their computers, deposited, and returned from his bank because of insufficient funds, he'll have the money to write the company a new one.

Ruth has yet another way. She's been using the same dry cleaner for several years. When things are tight, she postdates a check to pay for her cleaning. The owner doesn't mind holding it until it's good because she's a steady customer.

Ted sometimes deliberately puts the wrong checks into return envelopes—mixing up the checks to MasterCard and the telephone company, for example. That buys him another two weeks while the mixup is straightened out, by which time he can usually get the money into his account and cover everything.

No matter the form, it all comes down to the same thing: You write checks on funds you don't have.

Bouncing Right Along

Heather, who works in television production, holds the all-time record for bounced checks among people I know. Before she began this program, she bounced 201 checks in a single year. She made good on every one of them; but still, you could have played a game of handball with practically any check she wrote. She also paid her bank more than $1,000 in bad-check charges that year. That was in the early 1980s. Today, her charges would be close to $5,000.

Clearly, Heather's an extreme. *You* don't bounce more than twenty a year. Or ten. Or five or six. And everyone bounces a check now and then, don't they? No. Most people without a debt problem hardly ever do.

I Can't Keep Track of It All

You have only a vague idea of your various financial obligations and responsibilities. It's all too complicated to keep in mind. You have difficulty relating them to the funds that are actually available to you.

You don't know what it costs you each month to live, or how that stacks up against your income.

There's Always Someone

Your finances and bills are nettlesome, even upsetting, but you feel that you won't ever get into real trouble because there's always someone to turn to: your spouse, your parents, your brother, your sister, a good friend, someone you're close to who has money and who won't let you go under.

My good friend's name is Bob. He sent me a stock certificate to use as collateral when I was out of money and needed a $10,000 loan from Chemical Bank to live on while I finished a novel, and sent another certificate when I had to kick that loan up to $17,500, and later a personal check for $500. That accounted for $18,000 of my debt.

There's always someone.

But I Can't Do It Alone

You believe that for some special reason *you* are different, that *you* can't handle all these bills and obligations by yourself, that *you* need someone to help you.

- You're no good with numbers.
- You don't have a college degree.
- Women were never taught about money.
- You have a serious medical problem.
- *Your* expenses are extraordinary.
- Your field doesn't pay very much.
- You have too many responsibilities.
- You're only a couple of years out of school.
- You're too old.
- You're divorced, and you can't make it without your husband's income.
- You're divorced, and you have to pay alimony and child support.

Any reason will do. What counts here is that you *have* a reason; there's something about you or your situation that makes it impossible for you to avoid going into debt.

These are the most common warning signs of a serious problem with debt. It's not necessary for all or even a majority of them to apply to you. I only hit a few myself; so do most others who are in trouble with debt. We're all unique, we each have our own personal styles, forms, and combinations.

How many times did you see yourself here?

Obviously, no one *wants* to have a problem with debt. And practically everyone's first response is to deny or justify it somehow. That's eminently natural: Who the hell *would* want this?

Debt can be extremely painful.

It's also wholly unnecessary.

Your debts, whether you believe it or not at this point, are not crushing or hopeless. They are only a problem—and one for which there is a solution. But no one ever eliminated a problem until they recognized, or admitted, that there *was* a problem. You can, if you work the Back to the Black program, put your debts behind you forever. In fact, you're already doing so. You began the moment you opened this book.

4

HOW WE
GET THERE

No one starts out overwhelmed by debt. It begins with a little one here, another one there, and pyramids, scarcely noticed—or even denied—until it's out of control. Sometimes the process takes years.

I probably borrowed a couple of bucks from friends for gas or a Coke and a hamburger when I was a teenager. Everyone did; I don't remember now. I do remember my first adult debt. It was the 1960s. I was twenty-two, living in Manhattan, and waiting for a check for a magazine article I'd written. I needed that money, and I needed it quickly. So I borrowed $500 from my father. During the next eight years I was sometimes in debt and sometimes not—when I was, it was usually for a couple of hundred or maybe $1,000 to credit cards or department stores.

There wasn't any noticeable problem, not then.

When I was thirty, I bought a house and moved out of New York City with my wife and two children up north into the Catskill Mountains. Within a month, the oil burner died and a violent rainstorm revealed that the roof was shot. The new oil burner was $350; the roof, $2,000. Buying a house and making the shift from urban to rural living had eaten up most of my reserves. I bought the oil burner and arranged with my roofer to give him $1,000 up front and pay off the balance at $100 per month.

From that day on, I was never completely free of debt. The amount waxed and waned in response to the vagaries of my income and events of my life. It generally varied between $2,000 and $10,000. Somehow, there was never quite enough money. The house needed work, the kids were growing, there was always another insurance premium, I renovated my studio, checks from publishers were delayed, my oldest son was precocious and went to college early. There was always something, always a new need to borrow.

A novelist's income is sporadic. Long periods of time frequently pass between checks. The system that seemed to evolve of its own accord was this: I'd get a big check in, wipe out the major debts, and use the rest to live on for the next couple of months. Then I'd run out of money and begin borrowing again until the next check, and the cycle would repeat itself. Uncomfortable as it sometimes was, it worked for a long time. About thirteen years, actually. When it finally collapsed, I found myself $50,000 in debt, with a guaranteed income of only $350 per month, and expenses of $3,000 a month.

I didn't know what was wrong. I didn't know how it had all happened. There was only one thing I knew with certainty: I could not borrow any more money. I *could* have—there were people who would have loaned it to me—but though I didn't know what to do, I finally did know what *not* to do.

How to go about that was another matter.

My story is just that—my story. Each of the millions still suffering under crippling debt at this moment has his own story, her own story. So does each of the hundreds of thousands who have freed themselves from debt using the material in this program and who are now living happily, prosperously, and debt-free.

The Core of It

Before we can begin to deal with the ways to avoid new debt and liquidate existing debt, we have to understand just how we got into debt in the first place.

The core problem is simple: Repeated debt results from dysfunctional (or distorted) attitudes and perceptions about money and self. They are generally subconscious; we don't even realize they're there. Yet they rule our behavior and actions with the power of a dictator. It's essential to recognize them for what they are. Unless you do, no external event, no influx of money, no matter how large, is going to correct your financial situation.

In this chapter we'll cite the most common and destructive ones. Everyone is different. Everyone has his or her own style; only some of the following will apply specifically to you. But any combination of them, or even a single one operating in your subconscious with sufficient strength, can propel you headlong into debt despite your best conscious efforts to avoid it.

I Don't Understand Money

You might think you don't understand money, but that's not true. What you don't understand is the world economy. Neither does anyone else. Or maybe it's the complexities of high finance you don't understand. Not many do.

Forget about economies, forget about subordinated debentures and cotton futures.

Money is nothing but a medium of exchange. It's a symbol. You give your employer time (work), and he gives you money. You give your retailer money (value), and he gives you a television set. That's all there is to it. There's no mystery or magic about money. Its function is simply to make life easier. I don't have to haul around my herd of cows or wagons of salt when I want to buy something; I can give you currency or a check instead.

When you confuse your personal money with the science of economics and the business of finance, you complicate the issue so badly it becomes a source of intimidation and fear. You tell yourself you can't possibly understand it, that it's hopeless to try, that it's all the province of other people.

That's not true: Anyone who has mastered grade school arithmetic or who can push the buttons on a simple calculator has all the technical mastery she needs to understand her personal money.

When the Going Gets Tough, the Tough Go Shopping

You use money as a mood-changer. You go shopping, you buy and spend not for any realistic reason, but on an emotional basis.

Toni feels blue. She's listless and low-energy, nothing seems worthwhile. She can't break out of it. "Go buy yourself something pretty," a friend tells her. "That'll cheer you up." So she goes downtown to Marshall Field's and charges a $150 silk blouse, a $70 skirt to go with it, and $40 worth of cosmetics, and sure enough, she feels a lot better.

Frank's divorced. He misses his kids. He's living in a studio apartment. It's empty and too quiet. He's begun to date again, but he's still lonely. He bought a new computer and powerful visual design software for $3,500 to give himself something to do on nights when he's home. It helped for a while. He spent $1,300 upgrading his sound system. He likes that, especially in the morning when he's getting ready to go to work. The weekdays are more or less okay, but weekends are hard. A change in environment might do it, he tells himself, and some new faces. So he calls his travel agent and signs up for a $1,700 cruise to the Caribbean.

Bob rarely feels lonely. He's active in sports and belongs to social organizations. But there's not much real love in his life. When awareness of that breaks through, he feels hollow and without purpose. But he knows how to make the emptiness go away—he goes out and buys a new suit and a couple of new ties, or some shoes, or replaces a piece of furniture. Last month, when the woman he was dating broke up with him, he went out and bought new skis, new boots, and an entire new wardrobe for the coming winter season.

Joanie is a graduate student. She works hard, particularly on papers and when she's preparing for exams. These periods are intense and grueling. She motivates herself by giving herself a reward as soon as she's finished. Three months ago it was new curtains for the bedroom, two months ago it was a pair of knee-high Italian boots, last month it was a DVD player.

Fran is frequently uneasy and anxious. She worries about her job, her lover, her mother's ill health. The lunchtime noise and hustle on the streets around her office building discomfort her. She dissipates these feelings by ducking into a store and buying something—anything, from a pen or music CD to a piece of costume jewelry or a kitchen appliance. She does this several times a week.

Ed is often bored. His job and life are pretty routine. There's not much in them to fire him up. He too shops and buys a lot. There's an element of thrill whenever he makes a purchase, and another when he brings it home and takes it out of the box. It breaks the monotony and perks him up.

When you use money this way, you're using it the same way other people use alcohol and drugs—to escape uncomfortable feelings, to change your mood.

Everyone has these feelings; no one likes them. Some ride them out, others try to change them. There are an infinite number of ways to change them—working out in a gym or calling a friend to go dancing, building a model ship or catching a movie. But when you consistently buy and spend to pull yourself out of depression, to solace yourself when you're lonely, as a substitute for love, as a reward, to escape anxiety, or to cure boredom, you're moving steadily toward debt.

I'm Entitled

For some reason, any reason in the world, life owes you. You deserve that designer dress. You're entitled to charge that vacation in Hawaii.

This is why you deserve it, this is why you're entitled:

- You sweat your tail off at the shop.
- You're home all day with two young children.
- You had a rotten childhood.
- You worked eighteen hours a day for practically nothing when you were an intern.
- You stayed married.
- You bought everyone else presents.
- You got divorced.
- You were sick.
- You met your deadline.
- You got fired.
- You got a raise.
- You went through an awful weekend with your parents.
- Your spouse doesn't understand you.
- Your daughter doesn't need orthodontics after all.
- You totaled the car.
- The government got their piece, you want yours.
- Your picture was in the paper.
- You've suffered a lot.
- Everyone else does it.
- You had to work over the weekend.
- You caught your lover in bed with someone else.
- Your dog had puppies.

- Life is tough.
- You were elected Phi Beta Kappa.
- We're all going to die anyway.
- It's a damn fine day.
- You're truly a good person.

The list is endless.

When you spend because you feel you're entitled, any reason on earth will do.

A Dime & a Sandwich

You're not worth much and you never were. You have little or nothing to show for your life. You're not intelligent. You don't have a lot of character. Other members of your family are embarrassed by you or feel sorry for you. You don't have drive. You can't stick with it. You're not qualified for much. Something's missing inside. You fake your way through.

At thirty-five, Peggy wasn't carrying a large debt when she began this program—less than $3,500. But she'd been in debt most of her adult life. She was living in a tiny studio apartment. Her possessions were shabby. She bought most of her clothes secondhand. Yet she had a master's degree in English and had taught at a university in her early twenties while she studied for a doctorate. She was an intelligent woman, but she had little belief in herself and no sense of self-worth. She left the university and drifted from job to job in a downward slide until she ended up where she thought she belonged—checking coats in a nightclub for $250 a week.

Subconsciously she had impoverished herself as a demonstration of her worthlessness. Minimal survival was all she thought she deserved.

It was difficult for her to recognize and accept what she'd

done to herself. Even after she began an upward climb in this program and had tripled her income, she continued to keep herself in reduced circumstances for nearly a year, spending her money on cabs, movies, and meals out, leaving herself nothing to show for it.

A subconscious belief that you're worthless results in self-sabotage. You screw up jobs and lose them. You quit before your salary is increased or before you can be promoted. You're comfortable working only for minimal wages. If you do have more money than is compatible with this belief, you spend it, either recklessly or compulsively, until it's gone and you're left once again with nothing but a dime and a sandwich.

Look at Me, Ma, I'm on Top of the World

Grandiosity and spending for status are high dives into a pool of red ink. There's nothing wrong with desiring the finest and best in life. But that has to be matched realistically against available funds. The Saab Turbo 9-3 Hatchback S is a terrific car. It also costs $47,500. If you need a new car and like the Saab, if you have the money and aren't carrying any debt, terrific—buy it and enjoy it.

But if you're burdened with debts and scrambling for money every couple of months, a Plymouth Neon at $15,500 will get you where you're going just as well. And spending $32,000 less is going to help you get out of debt sooner; and the sooner you're out of debt, the sooner you'll really be able to afford that Saab.

Harriet is a freelance consultant who achieved a major income breakthrough half a dozen years ago, jumping from $40,000 to more than $160,000 a year. Yet she's under heavier financial pressure today than she ever was before, and her total debt is much larger than it was.

She's frequently so agitated by dunning creditors that she can scarcely work. She gets depressed. She's frustrated and angry at clients who are late in paying her. Last year, it got so bad that she was subpoenaed to appear in court for failing to pay $2,800 in property taxes. Theoretically, the county could have seized her house and auctioned it off for back taxes. Every asset she had was already pledged as collateral. All her credit lines were up to the maximum. No one would lend her another dollar.

Yet three months earlier, with the property tax bill sitting on her desk, she had charged a $4,900 vacation in Europe. And six months before that she'd bought a $36,000 automobile. She regularly throws lavish and expensive parties. Recently she told me that she always stays at the New York Helmsley when she's in New York. "Why should I stay in a $150-a-night room?" she asked. "I *like* $350-a-night rooms."

You spend on the biggest and the best, you pick up the tab at restaurants, buy silk blouses and imported shoes, join a trendy health club, own the latest electronic equipment, leave big tips, and vacation in the islands simply because, like Muhammad Ali, you're the greatest.

Money Corrupts

There is something inherently evil about money, right? Everyone who has it is corrupt. They're greedy, unprincipled, and insensitive. It's impossible for anyone who makes a lot of it to be an ethical or decent human being. It's cleaner, purer, and more virtuous and spiritual to live on the edge of poverty.

With this one lodged in your subconscious, you don't have a chance.

Question: How do you like to see yourself—corrupt, greedy, unprincipled, and insensitive; or as a decent, ethical human being? Any takers for corrupt, greedy, unprincipled, and insensitive?

So of course you're going to keep yourself in debt and out of money if to any degree you believe, as many do, that money is the root of all evil: It's a cleaner, purer, more virtuous, and more spiritual thing to do.

Actually, no one ever said that money is the root of all evil. The Biblical phrase, in the Book of Timothy, reads, "The love of money is the root of all evil." And the word *love* is used there in the sense of lust or covetousness.

There's an interesting variation on the idea that money corrupts: the belief that there isn't enough in the universe to go around. This tells you that whatever you have, it came to you at someone else's expense. It tells you that you can prosper only if someone else is deprived. Go outside and look around. Look up into the night sky. This is a rich and abundant universe. It's inexhaustible.

Money itself isn't even real. It's a fiction. You can't eat dollar bills. You can't build a house out of them. You can't burn them and keep yourself warm for very long. All wealth is the product of the human mind: Gold is a real substance, but it is valuable only because we *agree* that it is. It wasn't hamburger and potatoes that made millions for the founder of McDonald's, it was the *idea* of fast food.

Money itself is also neutral—neither good nor bad. You can raise a cathedral with money, you can build a death camp with it. What you *do* with it is up to you. You can become obsessed with acquiring money; you can become equally obsessed with avoiding it.

$200 Worth of Love, Please

You don't believe that people will love or appreciate you unless you buy them things or pay their way. Or you feel that you have to prove your own love by spending money on them.

This attitude can come into play in any situation.

- Your daughter's going to college. You love her and you want the best for her. Although a state school costs one-third as much, your love means Yale or M.I.T. for her, even if you have to go in hock up to the hilt.
- You've been working extra hard at the office and you haven't had the energy to go out and do things on the weekend with your wife. So when your vacation time finally arrives, you take her to Paris to make it up to her.
- It's the holiday season. Everyone's excited. You love them all—your children, your spouse, your parents, your brother and sister, your good friends. So you buy them gorgeous and expensive presents because you know how happy they'll be and you want to show them how much you love them.
- You never visit anyone without bringing a gift.
- You buy drinks for everyone.
- You can't spend as much time with your children as you'd like or think you ought. So you buy them things and give them a big allowance.

One way or another, you believe that love equals money.

Waiting for Godot

You're waiting for, wishing for, or planning on The Big Fix. It's going to clear your problems away and make everything better. As soon as it's here, you'll pay off all your debts, or at the very least have enough to handle everything on a monthly basis.

· · ·

You're going to:

- Get a raise
- Make a big sale
- Receive a gift from your grandmother
- Pick up the annual bonus
- Make a killing in the market
- Sell your stamp collection
- Receive an inheritance
- Graduate and go to work
- Sell the movie rights
- Win an insurance case
- Bring in an oil well

The Big Fix rarely arrives. If it does, it doesn't fix anything at all. The money is either already owed or it just buys a little more time. Sooner or later you end up in the same place again.

In my own case, I'd been living with my wife and children on $30,000 a year. It was the mid-seventies. One of my novels was optioned for film, was selected by several book clubs, and sold very well. That summer I received a royalty check for $50,000. By the time I paid off all the significant debts, celebrated a bit, and undertook some renovations on the house, there wasn't much left. A year later, life was pretty much what it had been before. I was back in the cycle of borrowing and paying off, borrowing and paying off.

The Big Fix is a contemporary deus ex machina. In classical Greek drama, the plot often compounded to a point where everything seemed hopeless and incapable of resolution. Then thunder would clap and a crane-like device would lower an actor playing one of the gods down to the stage. The "god" would intervene and set everything right. This was the deus ex machina, or "god from a machine"— The Big Fix.

The Big Fix happens in drama, not life. And not always in

drama either. In Samuel Beckett's *Waiting for Godot,* the characters' focus is on another character, named Godot, whose imminent arrival is going to have a major impact on their lives.

Godot never shows up.

But you keep waiting for him.

It's All Going to Go Away

You refuse to spend money. You let go of it only under duress or when absolutely necessary.

How can that lead to debt? You've got to be a freewheeling spender to become a debtor, right? You have to be propelled by a sense of entitlement, grandiosity, or one of the other gushers, don't you? How in God's name can you go into debt when you're hanging on to every dime as if it were the last morsel of food on earth, when someone practically has to point a gun at your head before you'll buy or spend anything?

Easy. Let's look behind this clenched-fist syndrome. If you ate the last morsel of food on earth, what would happen? There would be no more food left. And you would starve to death. But as long as you hang on to what you've got, there's still one more meal left to you.

The underlying perception is: There is not enough for you. This is a siege mentality, a bomb-shelter vision. You have to survive on whatever supplies you now have. Nothing more will come in. You're going to run out, and then what will happen? Where will you live, what will you eat?

What has happened is that you have become an anorectic spender—any amount you spend is too much. Each time you must spend—for rent, for medical treatment—you become depressed and upset. You spend only on what is absolutely essential for survival. You ceased long ago to spend on anything that gives you pleasure or improves the quality of your life—you'd never buy fresh flowers, for example, or join a gym, go to the theater, buy new, attractive, and well-made clothes. These are all frivolous luxuries. You're almost incapable of even thinking about them.

This leads inevitably to feelings of impoverishment and deprivation. And nearly as inevitably, those feelings lead to underearning and debt; like begets like, and when you expect the worst, you eliminate the alternatives. Since your perception tells you there isn't enough, you have to borrow to get through. This means you go deeper into debt, and now there is even less. So you borrow yet again, and fall still further behind. Your life is in constant retreat, your circumstances ever reduced. You see fewer and fewer options. Opportunities close down. Income declines to a level of minimal survival, or even lower, where you become dependent on others.

Anorectic spending, with its underlying siege mentality, strips the happiness and pleasure from your life piece by piece until there is nearly none left. Without happiness or pleasure, you grow even more despairing and fearful and cling all the more tightly to the money you do have left.

Increasingly, this blocks the flow of new money into your life. Money is not static. It needs open channels through which to flow. When you congest it this way, when all your energies and focus are given over to defending what you do have, you prevent more from coming in to you.

Women Can't Handle Money

Everyone knows women don't have the head for money. Most make a great meat loaf but they couldn't add two and two together if their lives depended on it. Is there anyone out there who still buys that? Refutation should be unnecessary, but for those who'd like an example or two: My agent is a woman, so is one of the best accountants I know, and so are a lot of portfolio managers on Wall Street.

However, there's a new contemporary version of this that goes: "I, as a woman, was never *taught* about money. Therefore," runs the corollary, "I can't handle money." And therefore, runs the result, you go into debt.

Scarcely anyone in this country *was* taught about money, about their personal money. You can prove this easily to yourself. Poll the people you know who don't have a debt problem, especially the women. Ask them if they were ever taught about money in school or by their parents. You're not likely to find more than one or two, if any, who'll say yes.

To repeat: There's no mystery or magic about money. Anyone who mastered grade school arithmetic or can use a simple calculator is capable of managing his or her own personal finances.

It's the belief, hidden or not so hidden, that you as a woman can't handle money that's causing the trouble.

I'm a Special Case

This is all well and good for other people, but *you're* different. It's impossible for *you* to avoid debt or to get out of it because of a unique situation or set of circumstances.

You, it must be seen, are different, because you're an:

- Actor
- Small-business owner
- Consultant
- Ski instructor
- Secretary
- Jack-of-all-trades
- Clergyman
- Graduate student

- Writer
- Unskilled laborer
- College professor
- Medical intern
- Policeman
- Photographer
- Librarian
- Father of five
- Unemployed
- Chimney sweep
- Waiter
- Artist
- Medieval scholar
- Butcher
- Baker
- Candlestick maker
- Alien from another planet

Or because you're:

- Old
- Young
- Black
- Hispanic
- A woman
- A genius
- A slow learner
- In a wheelchair
- Frightened
- Contentious
- Ignorant
- An ex-con
- Self-made
- Inexperienced
- A specialist

Or too:

- Beautiful
- Homely
- Tall
- Short
- Fat
- Thin
- Loved
- Unloved
- Hairy
- Bald
- Just plain weird

Anyone can come up with a reason why he is different, why he can't avoid debt or get out of it. The point is, you *have* a reason. But no matter how exotic your situation, there are others who share it who do not have a debt problem.

Good People Help Others

Your son is buying his first house. Your brother's down on his luck. Your best friend is between jobs. Your elderly parents are living on a fixed income. They need your help. Not only is it moral to help them, but you *want* to help them.

So even though you can't afford to, you give them money: because you want to, because you think you ought to, because you believe they'll suffer if you don't or that they can't make it without you. You do this even when you have to take out a loan yourself to make it possible.

Your motivation is kind, generous, and unimpeachable—but when you're carrying heavy debts yourself, when money is tight, that is not generosity but a self-destructive act. It's true that you can't love someone else if you don't love yourself; it's also true that you can't help anyone else with money if you can't help yourself. If you're financially responsible for children or others, the single most important thing you can do for them is create financial soundness for yourself.

You might be able to bail someone out a few times while you're in debt yourself, but that's only going to worsen your own situation, and next time, or the next, when someone truly needs you, you won't be able to help.

The Organ-Grinder's Monkey

You remain consistently underemployed or underearning. You've told yourself you're incapable of doing anything more difficult or demanding than what you're already doing. Or that you're not worth any more than what you're already being paid.

It's fate, the stars. Here you are and here you'll stay, forever, a chained monkey with a tin cup, begging for nickels. "That's life," you say, believing it and therefore creating it.

Yeah, but I Still Want to Be a Kid

It was nice when you were a child. Everything was provided, and through no efforts of your own, as if by magic. You still want it to be that way. You want to be taken care of. You want your parents to bail you out, your sister to help pay the rent, the government to pay the doctor's bill, your husband to buy you a car, your wife to handle the money. You want someone else—anyone else—to do it for you.

Monsters in the Dark

These are nightstalkers. They are bogeymen. You don't name them, you won't allow them into your conscious thoughts. But they're there nevertheless, haunting your dreams and patrolling the borders of your life, keeping money out and away from you.

You're afraid of:

Success This is startlingly common. You fear that you can't handle the increased responsibility success would bring; that you'd fold up under pressure. You know, somewhere within, that you're a fraud. If you move up too far, the eye of scrutiny will fall upon you. You'll be exposed. It's safer right where you are. You won't be noticed, you won't be found out. You know you could never cope with fame or wealth. It would make you crazy and you'd only hurt yourself with it.

If you were successful, you'd lose your friends and even the people you love. They'd envy you. They'd resent you. They'd be suspicious and afraid of you, wouldn't want to be around you anymore. Success would place demands on you that you have neither the energy nor ability to meet. You'd have to change your style of life, and you wouldn't know how to do that. Success would mean you'd surpass your parents, and that would mean their overthrow and betrayal, that you are an unloving and ungrateful child. It would disqualify and demean their lives and consign them to impotency, helplessness, old age, and an unhappy vision of their own achievements.

Failure You cannot tolerate failure. Therefore, you never put yourself in a position where that's possible. You globalize failure, seeing it not as a single incident, but as a pattern throughout your life: "I never win. I never get what I want. I always mess it up. Nothing ever works out for me." You see failure as condemnation.

You're a perfectionist, with an all-or-nothing vision. If you're not perfect, then you're worthless. If your work isn't perfect, it might as well be thrown out. If you don't blow the interviewer out of her chair, then you blow the interview. If you can't be president, there's no point in being account executive. The result is, you won't try anything unless you're absolutely certain you can do it.

You catastrophize; that is, you magnify a setback or a negative event way out of proportion. You work up the courage to try something new, your superior rejects it, and you view that not simply as one try that didn't pan out, but as a colossal rejection and a judgment upon your entire life.

Independence You don't want to be autonomous and self-reliant. If you are, then what will happen if something really big hits you and you can't handle it? You'll go down, that's what. There won't be anyone else there to prop you up. You know deep inside, no matter what others think, that you really can't take care of yourself. Even worse, if you *were* independent, then not only would you have to take care of yourself—which you can't—but others might become dependent on you, and then what would you do?

Did you see yourself reflected in this chapter? If you did, it's not surprising. I found myself here. So did every one of the hundreds of people in debt with whom I've spoken over the last eighteen years, and the hundreds of thousands more who've worked their way free with this program over the past decade and a half. And I'd lay odds that every one of the millions more who are struggling against debt across the country at this moment would see themselves here too. If they didn't, I'd be astonished. And skeptical.

The first clear look at what's really been going on in your subconscious can be a shock. You might feel dismal or depressed, or you might tell yourself it's hopeless. It isn't. In fact, seeing yourself here is the best thing that could have happened. It's a quantum leap in awareness of how you got into debt, and without such awareness there can be no change.

Regardless of how long or how powerfully these attitudes and perceptions have held sway over you, if you work this program, you can change them. That change won't take place overnight. It's a process. Some people require longer than others. But it *can* and *will* take place.

So what happens in the meantime? Are you condemned to keep going deeper into debt, to keep sweating until you begin to look at yourself and your money through different eyes?

No.

By using the concepts and the practical techniques and strategies in the following chapters, *you can bring your debting to a halt right now.* You can reverse your situation and begin to liberate yourself from debt immediately. You can do this despite the lingering presence of dysfunctional beliefs, despite the number of years you've been incurring debt, and despite the size of your total debt.

All you have to do is turn to the next chapter.

PART II

STOPPING THE DEBT SPIRAL COLD

5

The Concepts
of Change

You got into debt largely as a result of the distorted attitudes and perceptions, which led to destructive behavior patterns, that we discussed in Part I. Simple recognition—seeing them for what they are—is a big part of freeing yourself. They have no more real substance than shadows on a dark night; when you shine the light of conscious awareness on them, you begin to neutralize them. The rest of the job is to replace them with healthy and realistic visions.

The practical techniques and strategies you'll use to free yourself from debt begin in Chapter 6. Here we need to discuss some of the less tangible but equally important parts of the program. You need to be at least familiar with the following concepts before you can begin to take effective action. There's nothing Pollyannish about them, no matter how they may strike you at first. If you feel doubt or resistance, that is simply a measure of how strongly entrenched your old ways of thinking are. These concepts are all grounded solidly in a reality. Read them carefully. Think about them. Establish them firmly in your mind. Work with them each day. Use them as guidelines, let them inform and influence your emotions and decisions.

Right Now, You're Perfectly All Right

Right now, at this very moment, you have:

1. A roof over your head
2. Clothes to wear
3. Food to eat

So right now, today, you are perfectly all right—you have everything you need, you don't lack for anything essential.

Simplistic? No. Simple? Yes.

Alex works in public relations. He was $65,000 in debt and financially paralyzed when he began this program. His emotions were chaotic and his marriage was in trouble because of debt. Two and a half years later, he now meets all his monthly obligations without difficulty, his lifestyle includes such restored amenities as vacations, theater, and dining out. He's much calmer, his marriage is strong again, and he has liquidated $31,000 of his debt. In his words, "This is a simple program for complicated people."

Right now, today, you're perfectly all right. You have everything you need. This is an anchor stone. Take a minute to do the following:

Close your eyes. Breathe deeply a couple of times. Relax your body and clear your mind. Ground yourself in this day, which is where you belong. It's not yesterday. It's not tomorrow. It is today. Picture the roof over your head. Today, at this moment, you are not living out in the elements. Visualize the clothes you're wearing. See the clothes that are in your closet, in your bureau drawer. Realize that today, right now, you do have clothes to wear. Now picture what you had for breakfast, what you had for lunch, for dinner. Connect with this. You have had, and you do have, all the food you need today.

Consider that, and know this to be absolutely true: Right now, today, you have a place to live, clothes to wear, and food to eat.

Yesterday's gone, tomorrow isn't here yet. All that is real, ever, is today. And right now, today, you are perfectly all right. You have everything you need.

It's good to go through this process every morning. Shortly after you wake, before you get out of bed, sit for a minute or two, close your eyes, and visualize these things. It's a great way to start your day, knowing that you're perfectly all right and that you have everything you need.

At intervals throughout the day, take a few minutes to do the exercise again, especially if you begin to worry about or get depressed over bills and debts. Those emotions come because you're projecting into the future. You're responding to what you think is going to happen next week, next month, next year.

You don't know what's going to happen. Nobody does, nobody possibly can. So, in truth, all you're reacting to is your own imagination. There is nothing real in that. Slow down when this occurs. Stop. Go off by yourself to a quiet place. Close your eyes and do this visualization exercise.

Focus on today. Right now, today, is where you live. *And right now, today, you are perfectly all right.*

You Are Not Your Bank Balance, You Are Not the Sum of Your Debts

You are a human being. Human beings are a combination of many elements—physical, intellectual, emotional, and spiritual. You are a parent, a child, a lover, a friend. You are connected to a great many people by a variety of emotional ties. You laugh when you encounter something funny. You cry when you are moved. You are stirred by beauty. You love, and you are loved.

You create, you do, you think, and you feel. Your worth and value, to God or the universe, are precisely the same as any other human being's. Numbers are an invention of man.

So is paper. Numbers on a piece of paper are not your reality. Your heart, your mind, your soul are your reality.

Who is Frieda?

"$6,700 cash assets, $9,600 liabilities."

That's absurd.

You are not your bank balance, you are not the sum of your debts.

You're Not Living for Your Creditors

MasterCard is prohibited by law from owning human beings. So is Citibank. No institution may legally own anyone. Not even the IRS.

Nor can your brother or your best friend; the law won't allow people to own anyone either.

Yet most people in debt are living to one degree or another for their creditors, many as if they were wholly owned by them. Every dollar they earn that's not earmarked for basic needs is turned over to a creditor. Their creditors have become the largest figures on their emotional landscape, juggernauts that dwarf everything else, crushing out pleasure, hope, joy, and happiness.

Your debts may have become objects of obsession. If that has happened, they're poisoning your life, sucking the color out of your days, haunting your sleep. Their voice is never far from your ear, and their demand is relentless. They grind away at your self-esteem and your sense of your own worth every day. Remember:

> *Your Creditors Do Not Own You.*
> *You Owe Them Money, Not Your Life.*

Your primary responsibility is to yourself, *not* to anything or anyone else. You are as fundamentally deserving of and entitled to as much happiness as any other person on this planet.

Neither God nor the universe has decreed that your soul has been reduced to second-class status and your rights stripped away because you owe $5,100.50 to the Pittsburgh First National Bank.

Paradoxically, the more you begin to live for yourself again, and the more you claim your rights to life, liberty, and the pursuit of happiness—which are not simply legal rights, but your birthright—then the more quickly, as a result of your new vision and approach to life, money will begin to flow your way, the more effectively you'll manage the money you already have, and the more rapidly you'll liquidate your debts.

You're not living for your creditors. This is your life, not theirs.

This Isn't a Rehearsal

You're eating, breathing, talking, loving, and living right now. This is your life, not a rehearsal. Life doesn't begin after you've paid off your creditors. This is it. Now.

You might have subconsciously fallen into a state of suspension because of your debts and put your life on hold—ceased to engage in most of what enriches it, enhances it, and makes it worth living. If so, you hardly ever play anymore. Your level of physical activity has declined. There's not much time for reading. You rarely take a simple walk. You don't stretch out on the couch and listen to music. Pure relaxation and simple recreation, for their own sake, are largely things of the past.

At one extreme, you may have become a workaholic, with neither time nor energy for much else, your central focus the struggle to keep your creditors at bay and stave off the catastrophe of going broke for one more week, one more month. Or, just the opposite, you may have been overcome by lethargy, listlessness, procrastination, depression, and the sense that any task at all requires monumental effort.

Either way, the result is the same: You have deferred real living, pleasurable engagement with life, until some future date when all your debts have been paid. But it's not going to begin when you've liquidated your debts. No one's going to throw a switch then. *This isn't a rehearsal*. It's your life, right now. And the fact that you are in debt does not obligate you to suffer today.

Feelings Aren't Facts

Your emotions are simply that—emotions. They are not facts. They are not evidence of the way things really are. They are, in fact, little more than reflections of your own thoughts and perceptions. You may, for example, *feel* that your problems are overwhelming and hopeless, but that doesn't mean that they *are* overwhelming and hopeless.

This is an important distinction. It is appropriate to feel fear if a large, savage dog lunges through an open gate at you; or grief at the death of a loved one. But most fear and despondency stem primarily from your cognitions, from what you *think*. Ancient sailors experienced fear when storms blew their ship far out to sea. They became afraid they would fall off the edge of the earth. Despite the intensity of their fear, which was generated entirely by what they *thought* might happen, they were not going to fall off the edge. Their emotions were simply that—emotions. They did not reflect the actual facts.

Like countless others, I felt devastated by my debts. I was waking up each morning with ground glass in my stomach. My first conscious thought was, "Oh Christ, there's another bill coming in today. I'll never be able to pay it." I felt overwhelmed, hopeless. I lived under constant pressure, and was certain there was no way out.

But those were emotions. They reflected nothing but my thoughts and perceptions. They did not reflect reality.

When a negative emotion sweeps over you, don't try to repress it or crush it by brute force of will. That's not very effective. Instead, acknowledge that it's there and allow yourself to feel it for a minute or two. It's never as bad as you're afraid it will be, once you recognize that all it really is, is an emotion. Then objectify it—make it a voice that's speaking to you from somewhere outside you—and say to it, "Thanks very much for sharing. But all you are is an emotion. You don't reflect reality any more than you would if you told me I was going to fall off the edge of the earth."

Remind yourself several times each day that *your feelings are not facts.*

Debt Is Nothing but a Temporary Situation

Your height is a permanent condition. So is the color of your eyes. Your debt is not. It's a situation. Situations are temporary. A cold is a situation. You didn't always have it, you won't have it forever. Debt is nothing more than that.

You're not going to incur one more dollar's worth of debt. You're going to pay each and every one of your creditors in full, and you'll do it comfortably, without depriving yourself. You're going to live the rest of your life in prosperity and abundance and free of debt forever.

Vivian is a spirited woman in her seventies who's been prominent in the fashion industry for many years. She had one of the larger debt structures—number of creditors and total amount owed—I've personally encountered: $240,000. And that was more than fifteen years ago. In today's dollars, she would owe $390,000. When I met her, she was completely hysterical. The IRS was on the verge of seizing

her co-op, she was months in arrears on maintenance payments, her desk was piled with bills and past-due notices,
and several of her creditors were threatening lawsuits.
She'd lost weight, had deep circles under her eyes, and
could scarcely hold food down. She'd begun to sell off family heirlooms to keep her creditors at bay. We talked for two
hours that day. She broke down and cried several times. She
knew it was hopeless. That's what her emotions told her,
anyway.

I remember clearly a call she gave me four years later. She
had just come back from Spain (a vacation for which she had
paid cash). She was still in debt then, but had paid off
$160,000 of it and owed only $80,000. She still owned her
apartment. Her creditors were receiving regular monthly
checks from her. They hadn't bothered her once in the previous two years. She was living better, not worse, than she
had in the old days. Today, completely free of debt for nearly
a decade, she lives better and with greater happiness and
peace around money than she ever did before.

Nancy, a social worker, was down $13,000. She's been
debt-free for the last two years.

Three years ago, Frank, a cabinet maker, couldn't meet
the rent on his shop and was about to give it up. He was
$50,000 in debt, and that was rising each month. In despera-
tion, he'd begun to sell off tools he needed to work with. Following this program, he stabilized within six months, upped
his income substantially, and has reduced his total debt by
$14,000 so far.

Debt is nothing but a temporary situation.

The Cavalry Has Arrived

Godot may not show up, but the cavalry will; in fact, it's
already here. You're the cavalry—you just didn't know it.

Vivian isn't going to get you out of debt. I'm not either. Nor is Nancy, or Frank, or anyone else. You are. Every tool you need is in your hands right now.

The concepts, techniques, and strategies in this book have been forged out of the combined experience of hundreds of thousands of people who have already gone before you. They have been tested, refined, and *proven* by men and women from every walk of life and background imaginable. I have never seen anyone fail who has worked the program with commitment.

You are the cavalry. And the cavalry has already arrived.

You've Got More Than You Think

The fact that you don't have everything you want doesn't mean that you have nothing. When you've come to focus obsessively on your debts, it's as if a filter has been placed over your eyes, and all the things you have and all that is good in your life fade out and then disappear. You no longer see anything but your debts, and they become exaggerated and monstrous.

This happened to me during the final two years of my debting. It progressed steadily until my life seemed composed almost entirely of deprivation and pressure.

I remember vividly an afternoon I was out walking with a friend. She stopped short and said, "Do you know what you just did?"

I said, "No. What?"

"I said, 'Look at the way the sun is coloring the clouds. Isn't that beautiful?' And you looked up for about half a second and said, 'Yeah,' and then you looked back down and said, 'I don't know what the hell I'm going to do. I've got a cap falling out, but I don't have the money to go to the dentist. I can't even make the rent next week.' Every time I've seen you in the last few months, all you've talked about is bills and money."

And she was right.

There was much about my life that was positive and good then, but I had lost sight of nearly all of it. I had, for example, largely recovered from an unexpected and painful divorce. I had two healthy and fine sons whom I loved and who loved me. I was living in Greenwich Village, which is a pleasant place to live. I had good friends. I was in better physical condition than I'd been in for years. I had a well-developed talent I could exercise as a craft, an art, and a career. I'd achieved a fair amount of popular and critical success over the years and my professional reputation was strong. I had a good relationship with an attractive and emotionally generous woman. . . .

There was quite a bit more, ranging all the way down to such smaller but not insignificant details as my increasing cooking skills, a color television and a VCR, an invitation to spend time out of the city with friends who had a summer home in the country. But I could see none of that then. All I could see were my debts.

No matter how pressured or impoverished you perceive yourself to be, realize that you have much, much more in your life that is good and pleasurable—right now—than you've led yourself to believe. Chapter 15 provides a formal exercise that will help you to accomplish this; for now, as a beginning, take a minute or two to move your gaze slowly about the room you're in (if you're not home, do it mentally). Pause, one at a time, for several moments at different objects you own that you enjoy owning. Consider each in turn, and feel your pleasure in them. You'll discover that *you have more than you think.*

It's Not Armageddon

The missiles won't be launched. Blood isn't running in the streets. You owe some money, that's all. You're not going to be shot at dawn. There is no debtor's prison.

Your debts don't mean anything more than that you owe some people some money. No one has drawn up articles of condemnation against you. You won't be dragged through the streets in a dunce hat and pelted with garbage. Your picture hasn't been tacked up in post offices. You're not wandering weary, friendless, naked, and hungry from village to village.

Catherine, a freelance editor with whom I was passingly acquainted, called me one afternoon weeping and barely coherent. She *had* to see me. She was desperate. We met in a park twenty minutes later. She was distraught and haggard. She'd called, she finally managed to say, after an hour of standing in front of a window in her seventh-floor apartment, thinking about jumping.

She called me because she'd remembered hearing from a mutual friend that I'd once been in serious trouble with debt myself, but that I'd turned everything around.

Catherine was $58,000 in debt—to credit cards, department stores, friends, the IRS, the state tax bureau, and her landlord. Her daughter's college tuition was due. She had just received an eviction notice. The pressure had been building a long time. She had no assets left, no one would extend her any more credit. The eviction notice was the final blow.

To her, Armageddon had come. And she almost killed herself: because she owed someone money. That's how badly the pressure of debt had distorted her vision.

Six months have passed. Catherine combined the concepts of this program with the practical techniques, which begin in the next chapter, in her own particular way, as everyone does. From that first day she hasn't gone one more dollar into debt. Her daughter is still in school. She has paid each month's rent, kept abreast of all her current bills, and reduced her arrears to her landlord by $2,900. She's reached agreement with most of her creditors and is still negotiating with the rest.

Was it easy? No. But most of her pain is gone now, and the last of the fear is receding. She's astonished that she was once on the edge of suicide. Her income is increasing. She's bought some new clothes and joined a gym. She recently took a weekend holiday in the mountains. Simply put, she has stopped debting—has begun the process of getting out of debt—and is beginning to enjoy her life again.

It wasn't Armageddon for Catherine.

It isn't Armageddon for you. It never is. You owe some money, that's all. And only for a while.

There Is No Tomorrow

Yesterday's gone. Tomorrow isn't here yet. It makes no difference what you did last week, last month, last year. That's history. Nor does it matter what's going to happen next week, next month, next year. No one knows that.

All that is real is today. Keep your focus, your thoughts, your emotions, in today. Keep them in the Now. *And right now, today, you are perfectly all right.*

6

LAYING
THE FOUNDATION

The practical techniques and strategies of the Back to the Black program, which begin in this chapter, are powerful in their own right. But if you try to use them out of context you'll handicap yourself, like trying to play a ball game with only half a team. The preceding chapters laid important groundwork. You need to be familiar with it. So if you haven't read those chapters, go back and do so now. If you have, you might want to review them and fix the material there freshly in your mind.

Some of the techniques in this book may seem nearly impossible to you at first. They did to me and many others. But they're not. There is *always* a way to succeed at them. You might find other techniques difficult and even painful in the beginning—scarcely anyone gets through the early stages without some degree of discomfort. You'll probably experience moments of doubt too. But all that will pass, like the soreness and aches that follow your first workouts in a gym; each day you grow stronger and more limber, and eventually you hardly remember the early difficulties at all.

Keep this in mind too: Any temporary discomfort you may feel is nowhere near the level of anxiety, pain, and despair that sooner or later overtakes everyone who continues to sink deeper into debt.

Finally, the rewards you'll win by working this program are enormous, far beyond your capacity even to imagine at this moment. The improvements in the quality of your life will be remarkable, just as they have been for me and everyone else.

Don't Shoot, I Surrender

It Is Absolutely Necessary to Accept That You Have a Debting Problem.

Without such acceptance, you'll only be applying Band-Aids. There will be no real change. It doesn't matter what you call yourself—problem debtor, compulsive debtor, or something else. Call yourself a Goodtime Charlie, if you prefer, a freewheeling spender, one of the nicest people in town, Sally who's sweeter than honey; hell, call yourself nothing at all if that makes you happier.

But, alone, in a quiet private place, surrender: Admit to yourself that you have a debting problem, and that it's caused a lot of pain and trouble in your life. Do it now. Okay. Take a couple of deep breaths and relax. Now try it again. Let it settle in. Let yourself feel the truth of it: You have a debting problem. It has caused a lot of pain and trouble in your life.

Many people experience a sense of relief when they finally admit this to themselves. I was one of those. My immediate response was: Thank God! Now I know what the problem is. Which means that I can fix it. Others react quite differently. They panic and bolt for the door, or want to punch out whoever made the suggestion.

Noreen, a writer and illustrator of children's books, attended one meeting of a group of people who work this program. She was nervous and fidgety through the hour and a half. At the end, she was literally backing toward the door as she spoke. "I can't deal with this," she said. "I just can't. My heart's pounding. I'm hyperventilating. I feel like I'm going to faint." She ran off into the night.

She was gone a year, then came back. This time she committed to her recovery, despite her fear. That was five months ago. She stopped debting immediately. She started to edge her income up; last month it was $480 higher than when she entered. The tension is slowly leaving her face.

Danny, a welder, came to four or five meetings. He remained silent through each one, mouth tight, face flushed with anger. Finally, he exploded in rage and stalked out. I run into him on the street now and then. I don't mention money; he never fails to.

"I know the program is right," he told me the last time I saw him. "But it makes me crazy, it makes me want to smash things. I can't face it. Maybe when it gets so bad that I just can't take it anymore, maybe then I can do it."

That's the way it is with some people. They have to be pushed right up against the wall, and through it, before they'll admit what's going on. They have to be left with utterly no other choice. Panic and anger are natural responses. For most of us, surrender is an abhorrent word. It appears to violate everything we've been taught:

"Never say die."

"Damn the torpedoes, full speed ahead."

"I have not yet begun to fight."

Resistance to surrender, which stems from fear, is based largely on a misconception of what the word means. If you're like most people, you interpret surrender as losing freedom, being defeated, being weak. But one of its primary definitions is:

To Give Something Up
in Favor of Something Else.

It is simply letting go of an old way of doing things in order to embrace a new one. When you admit that you have a debting problem, when you surrender to that, you become willing to let go of your old perceptions and behaviors, which resulted in deprivation, pressure, and unhappiness, and in their place embrace new ones, which bring about freedom, ease, and thriving.

This surrender, paradoxically, is your first triumph.

Defusing Denial

Denial is the refusal to admit you have a problem. It's an attempt to rationalize or justify your debts, to assign responsibility to someone or something else. It is a wholly natural reaction. It's also a dangerous one. If you buy it, you're not going to have much success in stopping your debt spiral or in ever getting out.

Denial is nearly universal at first—after all, no one *wants* to have a debting problem. You tell yourself it's your parents' fault. It's the government's fault. Your wife's fault. The economy's fault, the patriarchy's, the banks', the credit card companies', your boss's fault, society's fault. It's the divorce, you say to yourself, it's the job market, late-paying accounts, taxes, interest rates, the new roof, high rents. Anything or anyone but you, even though you're the one who borrowed the money, who charged the goods and took the services.

Actually, it isn't your fault, not in the sense that you're flawed or that you did something wrong and are guilty and deserve punishment. You didn't plan this, you didn't deliberately set out to put yourself in this position. Neither did I or any of the other thirty million people who are standing right alongside you. There's no blame in this: It was not intentional. But denial is a serious problem nonetheless.

Glen, an actor with a good professional history, was never deeply in debt, but he'd carried some amount nearly all his adult life. That had crept upward little by little each year until, at the time he undertook this program, he owed

$15,000 and his increasing poverty mentality had eroded the quality of his life and damaged his ability to get work. For nine months he *appeared* to work this program—knowledgeably discussed its concepts at a support group, practiced some of its techniques—but his situation grew steadily worse. At the end of the nine months, he'd gone through the emergency grants his performers' unions had given him, there were no prospects of work, he had no money for rent, hardly enough for food, and creditors were threatening to haul him into court.

His face was anguished. His body seemed to be collapsing. "I'm beaten," he said. "I've had it. I've been trying to play the angles. I figured *you* people had the problem, not me. I was only here to take a scan and pick up a quick fix. It's over, I'm finished. My way doesn't work."

He surrendered that night, which he had never done before. That was eight months ago. This time he *worked* the program. He didn't have an easy time, but he stayed with it. Today he's working in a role on Broadway for $2,500 a week and gradually reducing the debt that once crippled him.

The turnaround begins with surrender to the fact that you have a debting problem—and denial can be as lethal to surrender as a bullet. To combat denial:

1. Freely admit it's there. Tell yourself that of course you'd rather not have the problem. Who would? But recognize that personal preference doesn't change the facts. I'd much rather be six-feet-two and have a full head of hair again. But I'm not, and I don't. I have preferences, but they don't change the facts.

2. Reread Chapters 1 through 5. Remember that the material within them isn't theoretical; it's been drawn from the lives of countless people who are in serious trouble with debt. Write down the number of times you find yourself there, to impress that fact upon yourself.

3. Remember you're not unique in having a debt problem. It doesn't place you with a tiny minority who somehow haven't been able to make things work. There are literally *millions* of Americans in precisely the same situation.
4. Drive home to yourself that surrender doesn't sentence you to poverty and a hard life—just the opposite: It's your first step on a road to freedom from that.
5. Proceed as if you *didn't* have any denial. Don't let it sidetrack you from your purpose. Denial is simply that—denial. It can't *force* you to do anything. You can go right ahead with this program despite its presence. In time, with repeated constructive action, its grip will loosen.

Sometimes denial goes dormant for a while, only to pop up again later. It often reappears when you've begun to reverse your situation and the stress is easing—or simultaneously with a large influx of money, from whatever source. The old attitudes and behavior patterns don't die easily. They may simply have gone into hiding, marking time, only to break into the open again at the first good opportunity.

Everyone has such moments. My own internal dialogue usually goes something like this: "You know, I really appreciate all the help and good wishes, and indeed it was quite useful, but I think there's been a misunderstanding here. You see, I was simply depressed after my divorce, it was a slow time in my career, I had some large responsibilities, and I made a couple of mistakes. That's really all there was to it. I'm fine now, so thanks a lot and all the best to you. I'll be moseying along now."

This kind of thinking is a one-way ticket right back to the place you started from.

Leo is a typical example. He's a salesman who usually earned about $60,000 a year and was $24,000 in debt. In four years of working this program, he successfully liquidated his debts and increased his income to $75,000. The problem was gone, he believed, so he didn't need the regimens of the program any longer. Within eighteen months he'd incurred $17,000 in new debt and was in a panic again. He undertook the program once more, has paid off half his debt in the past year, and this time swears he's sticking with the principles in this book for good.

If denial does resurface later and you're tempted to say, "Thanks, and so long," return to this section and go through the defusing procedures once more.

Bankruptcy Me No Bankruptcies

Bankruptcy is not an option.

Did you howl with shock and indignation when you read that? Some people do. Bankruptcy has been their ace in the hole. When it's really Alamo time, when the enemy's finally breached the wall and is charging in for the kill, they plan to bail out through bankruptcy. Zap! All your debts are wiped out with one stroke and you can start over with a fresh slate.

Easy. Pretty damn practical too, right?

Wrong.

Bankruptcy is just another version of The Big Fix. And like all the rest, it won't fix anything either. It'll buy you a little more time, that's all. Sooner or later—and usually much sooner—you'll end up in exactly the same kind of trouble you were in before.

The recidivism rate among people who declare personal bankruptcy, those who repeat it, now stands at higher than 50 percent, and continues to climb. That means that more than five out of ten people who declare bankruptcy will declare it again, and usually as soon as the law permits, currently six years. Bankruptcy changed nothing for them. They went right back to their old ways and started to debt again.

What about the others? Some probably *are* people who never really had a debt problem and were knocked over by a catastrophic event. And the rest are probably compulsive or problem debtors who returned to debting but still have some credit options left.

How can a bankrupted individual get back into debt? No one will give him credit, will they? Hell, numerous sources will. Certain finance companies advertise this blatantly in newspapers, on television, and even on posters in buses and subways. A bankrupt can borrow from friends and relatives. She can arrange time payments with providers of personal service. She can fall behind in rent and utilities. She can become delinquent in income and property taxes. Some stores, merchants, and even credit card issuers and other lending institutions are willing to extend her limited credit. She can parley up a sizeable new debt without much effort at all.

A recent television documentary included an astounding interview with a man named Craig, who had just declared bankruptcy. Craig, who is thirty-four, worked in restaurant supply and earned $48,000 a year. He was $40,000 in debt, mostly to the issuers of his many credit cards. Craig was happy as a clam. With zest and exuberance he told the interviewer that he was going right back to the same lifestyle. He'd discovered a great system, he said. Just keep racking up the debt, then declare bankruptcy every six years and wipe it out. He'd already spoken with new-car dealers. No problem, they told him, come in as soon as you have your final papers and we'll do business.

Clearly Craig has discovered a modern miracle. He doesn't have a problem anymore, right? Neither does a man tied to a stake in front of a firing squad—until the bullets reach him.

Anyone want to bet that Craig will make it through the next six years without his new debting eventually bringing him to a point where he's wiped out again and wandering around with the stunned and glassy look of someone who just survived the bombing of Dresden?

There are two forms of bankruptcy available to individuals, Chapter 7 and Chapter 13. Simplified: In the former, the bankrupt's assets are liquidated, the proceeds are given to his creditors, and his remaining debt is discharged. In the latter, he retains most of his property, repays as much as he can to his creditors over a period of, usually, three years—the amount determined by the court—and any debt remaining is discharged.

With one exception, bankruptcy is not an option, for these reasons:

- It does nothing to alter the beliefs and behavior that are the cause of a debting problem.
- It generally leads to a sense of failure, shame, and defeat, which only escalates the debting syndrome.
- It plagues your credit record for ten years (and can show up indefinitely in some situations), which may cause you difficulty later on, when in fact life may truly be going well for you.
- It encourages you to think that if things get tough you can always go that route again, which can destroy your opportunity to liberate yourself from debt and live free of it forever.

There is a further reason, too, for many people: they see bankruptcy as cheating the individuals and institutions who loaned them money in a good-faith business arrangement out of the return of their money.

The only reasonable exception to the argument against bankruptcy, at least for anyone with a history of debting, is when the situation is so complicated that bankruptcy offers relief while not—in reality—eliminating the debt. Here, the debt is not eliminated because the debtor, though his legal obligation is removed, remains personally committed to repaying it.

Ronnie, an entrepreneur in her late forties, exemplifies this principle. Ronnie owed $125,000 to more than thirty different creditors. She had tried hard to negotiate with them, but the situation was simply too difficult. So she informed each that she had decided to go bankrupt but that it was her intention to repay each of them in full as she was able. Which is what she did, over a period of nine years. Some of these creditors were so impressed they actually became sources of business referrals for her.

So if you've been thinking of bankruptcy as an escape hatch, put it out of your mind. It doesn't work, not for anyone with a debting problem.

A Month Without Worries

Starting today, right now, give yourself thirty days worry-free from debt.

You're entitled to this. You deserve it. In fact, you're likely to *need* it. You've been under heavy strain. You're probably worn down and exhausted. You're in no shape to do yourself—or your creditors—any good now. And to tell the truth, we don't give a damn about your creditors at this point: It's *your* life we're talking about, a decent life, a whole life, a happy life. The best thing you can do right now is to give yourself rest, give yourself respite and sanctuary, free from worry about your debts.

Here's how you do it. Sit quietly for a moment. Get comfortable. Close your eyes. Take a couple of deep, easy breaths, and relax. Let your mind go wandering through your house or apartment. What you're looking for is the friendliest container you can find. It should be one with which you have happy associations, one that gives you immediate feelings of well-being the moment your mind's eye falls upon it. It

might be a tackle box, a hat box, a box of old family photo-
graphs, or any similar thing. Have you found it?

Good.

Open your eyes. Get up and go get that box from wherever it is. Bring it to your desk and set it down. Sit with it for
a minute and think about all the good memories attached to
it. Experience the pleasant and comforting feelings it evokes.
You might even want to touch it or place your hands on it
while you do this, to strengthen your connection with it.

Now gather up every bill, past-due notice, and threatening communication from each of your creditors. Get them
all, every last one of them. Once you've done that, open your
friendly container. Place all the bills, notices, and letters inside it. Close the container. Bring it back to wherever it was
before and put it away.

Now: Forget about the bills and notices for the next thirty
days. This is important—truly *forget* about them. They don't
exist. They're not your problem. For now, they're God's
problem—let Him (or Her or It or the universe) worry
about them. He can handle it. Breathe a sigh of relief, then
go about your life and have a good time. You don't have to
think about these bills at all for the next thirty days; they'll
be there when you want them.

But what's going to *happen*? With a little luck, and a bit of
resolve, you'll have a good time, that's what.

I can't guarantee that you will. That's mostly up to you.
But I can guarantee this: The missiles won't be launched,
blood won't run in the streets, you won't be shot at dawn.

"But they're going to shut off my phone if I don't pay tomorrow!"

Most people with a debt problem can give themselves
this thirty-day gift of freedom without any negative effect
upon their situation whatsoever. If there is a critical exception, if the phone company really will shut off your phone
tomorrow—and don't kid yourself, be scrupulously honest
about this—then:

- Pay them whatever portion you can, as a token of good faith.
- Tell them that you acknowledge this obligation and that you're committed to paying it in full.
- Tell them that you just entered a financial recovery program and that you'll get back to them to discuss a repayment schedule next month.

They may not like this response, and may well express their dislike, but they'll probably go along with you. Then begin your thirty days.

"But I have to be in court tomorrow for nonpayment!"

Go ahead. Show up. Then begin your thirty days.

Let's assume you're at the midpoint of your thirty-day period now. Even though you're unaccustomed to such relief and it seems more than a little unnatural, you're actually enjoying your freedom. Then suddenly—whumph!—like a kick in the guts, an envelope from your most feared creditor arrives. This is it. You know what's inside. They're going to kill your cattle, burn your crops, and sell your children into slavery if you don't pay immediately.

What do you do now?

You could head up to the roof and think about jumping. But somehow, today, that no longer seems like a rational response.

Do not open the envelope. Take it directly to your friendly container. Open the container. Drop the envelope inside. That's where it belongs. Close the container. Walk away, forget about it, and continue your thirty days. It's God's job to worry about this stuff now, not yours.

You are tranquil again.

This time, the telephone rings. It's a collection agency. They want their money or they're going to sue. Be civil and be brief. Tell them exactly what you told the telephone company:

"I regret this situation. I acknowledge my obligation. I'm

committed to repaying you in full, and as quickly as is possible. My financial situation is difficult and unclear at this point. I have just entered a financial recovery program to correct this. I will be back in touch with you next month, on [give them a specific date], to discuss a repayment schedule."

Be firm. Remain calm and polite no matter how you may feel inside. Do not say anything else, do not agree to anything. As soon as you hang up, write the creditor's name and the date of the call on a piece of paper. Deposit it within your friendly container, then walk away, forget about it, and let God worry about it. It's His job for now, remember? Do what absolutely needs to be done to keep yourself from being seriously hurt, but nothing more.

That's it. Have the best thirty days you possibly can. You deserve them.

One Day

In the course of this chapter, you have laid a strong foundation on which to build your recovery. You have surrendered to the fact that you have a debting problem; taken steps against denial; recognized that bankruptcy is not a solution; and begun a thirty-day period free from worry about debt.

Here is a simple action you can take to complete your foundation work.

Just for Today, One Day, Do Not Incur Any New Debt.

Not one.

- Don't borrow $2 from a friend.
- Don't accept a service you plan to pay for later.
- Don't take a loan from a bank.
- Don't charge anything on your credit card.

This is easy. Anyone can do it. Just go through today, this one small twenty-four-hour period, without taking on any new debt in any form. No matter when you're reading this, and regardless of whether or not you've begun your thirty-day grace period or taken any other action, just do not incur any new debt today. If something is absolutely essential—which is rarely the case—find another, nondebting way to get it. Or defer it for twenty-four hours.

Fine. Now close this book, enjoy the rest of the day, and begin reading again tomorrow.

7

THE HEART OF IT

One Day at a Time

Congratulations! You didn't go one penny further into debt yesterday. You proved to yourself that it's possible not to incur a new debt for one day. In doing so, you have just accomplished the single most important part of the program.

This is the threshold:

Just for Today,
You're Not Going to Incur Any New Debt.

We're only talking about *one* day—today. Tomorrow is irrelevant. What you might do tomorrow, next week, next month, next year doesn't matter. They're not here yet. All that matters, all that is real, is today. And today, one day at a time, you're not going to incur any new debt.

Anyone can avoid debt for a single day. Thousands of people from every kind of life imaginable, who were once crushed by debt, have been proving this every day for nearly three decades. Today, right now, you have a roof over your head, you have clothes to wear, you have enough to eat. You have everything you need. You are perfectly all right. There is no reason for you to debt before this day ends. You can choose to do it, but you don't *have* to do it.

"But . . . !"

"But . . . !"

"But . . . !"

Right. Nearly everyone says that when the magnitude of this concept first strikes them.

"But I can't get my car out of the shop unless I use my credit card."

"But I don't have bus fare to get to work this morning."

"But I promised I'd take my mother out to dinner tonight."

For today, arrange a ride with a neighbor. For today, secure the loan of bus fare by giving your roommate a CD as collateral. For today, make dinner at home for your mother. Just for today, do not incur any new debt.

Here is a simple but profound truth:

You Can Not Get Out of Debt by Borrowing More Money.

No more than an alcoholic can become sober by having another drink.

One of my own "Buts" was: "But I have to get to the dentist. This cap keeps falling off. The root is broken. It has to come out. I need a bridge. And there's more work to be done too."

Ed, a tall, soft-spoken Southerner who worked in advertising, told me, "You're not getting the work done today, are you? Just don't debt today."

That was fine, I said angrily, but it was a front tooth, the work *had* to be done, and pretty soon too. Nearly $5,000 worth altogether. Just how the hell was I supposed to manage that without owing my dentist and paying him off over a long period of time?

Ed was unruffled. He'd been following this program several years and he'd seen this kind of reaction before. He knew I'd find an answer and he knew I'd change in time, that as I refrained from debting, my confidence in my own ability to find solutions would grow, my sense of crisis and catastrophe would abate, and my emotions would become steadier and more positive. These days—four years later— when I see that same raw panic and anger in someone else, I remain unruffled too. I know they'll find an answer, I know they'll change in time.

Ed suggested I sit down with a pad of paper and write out all the ways I could think of to get the work done without debting. "*All* the ways," he said, "no matter how off the wall any might seem." And he suggested I talk with others who'd faced a similar situation and ask how they had managed.

So what finally happened? I had the urgent work— enough to satisfy function and aesthetics temporarily—done at the New York University Dental School, where the cost was about a third of what a private dentist would have charged, and the rest by my own dentist through the following year, as I had the money. I paid for each stage on the spot, as the work was completed. I paid $3,500; that was $3,500 in new debt I didn't incur.

Ed said one other thing that afternoon, very casually. He said, "Miracles are commonplace in this program."

His words frustrated and angered me—I needed *help*, not platitudes. That was eighteen years ago: Miracles are commonplace in this program.

All you have to do to begin your recovery and open the door to total freedom is avoid taking on any new debt today. I don't avoid debt tomorrow, next week, next month, or next year. That's too much to think about. I just do it today, one day at a time. And these days, I have more prosperity in my life and enjoy it more than ever I did before.

It's vital to keep this principle firmly in mind. Tomorrow is irrelevant: *It's one day at a time.*

And just for today, for one day, you don't debt.

Some Practical Suggestions

You can probably see the logic and importance of not debting one day at a time. You're enthusiastic and ready to go, or maybe not so enthusiastic but at least willing to give it a try. Either way, just how do you go about that?

Several ideas might have occurred to you in response to some of your own "Yes, buts. . . ." However, once your initial flush of excitement passed, those answers might have begun to pale and look not quite so effective or plausible as they first did. Or you might have grown pessimistic as your old negative emotions came stealing back.

"Sure, I could probably make it for today, but let's be realistic, what happens tomorrow? What am I going to do next week when I have to pay the rent?"

It's just for today, remember? That's all we're ever talking about: one day, this day.

Pause here and relax for a few minutes.

Browse back through Chapters 4 and 5. Refresh your memory of the distorted beliefs and visions of yourself—"A dime and a sandwich," "I'm a special case," and all the others—that led you into debt, and of the new and healthy ones—"Right now, you're perfectly all right," "Feelings aren't facts," and the rest—with which you're replacing them.

Part of this program involves a change in consciousness, in the way you look at yourself and life. You'll be breaking through perceptual barriers that you or someone else placed in your way a long time ago, eliminating old restrictions in your thinking and striking out toward increasingly new and expanding horizons. This change has already begun: You don't think about yourself, debt, and money in quite the same way you did before you opened this book, do you? The process will escalate as you progress through the following chapters and as you work this program.

Right now, say the following to yourself. Say it out loud if

you're alone, or silently if there are others around. Say it
three times. Say it forcefully and with as much conviction
and belief as you can muster:

Countless Others Have Already
Freed Themselves from Debt.
I Am Just the Same as Them.
I Can Do It Too.
I Am *Doing It.*
I Am Doing It Now.

For the next month, sit quietly for a few moments before
you become involved in the activities of your day and reaf-
firm this. Repeat it strongly to yourself three times, out loud
if you can. And if at any time in the future you find yourself
wavering on this point, return to the practice each morning
for a week or two.

As you search for new options through which to bring in
more money or get what you need without debting, don't
permit false ego, fear, or an old dysfunctional self-image to
imprison your thoughts. Remember, you're breaking out of
old molds, you're reshaping old patterns. They don't work.
They're what brought you to this point.

Most of what passes for pride and ego actually stems from
a belief or fear that you're not really worth very much, that
you're a fake and barely able to hold things together. The
deeper these are, the more mightily you strive to prove to
yourself and the world that the opposite is true. No one, for
example, lights a cigarette with a $20 bill unless he's trying
desperately to convince himself and everyone else that he
isn't helpless and worthless.

As you refrain from debting one day at a time, as you
begin to prosper and liquidate your debts, you can not fail to
gain a true confidence in yourself and a genuine sense of
self-worth. If, for example, you brown-bag your lunch a couple of days instead of dropping $50 at a businessmen's

restaurant because that's what your fellow workers do, the self-esteem you'll quickly gain from beginning to take control of your finances will be much more powerful and meaningful to you than any possible loss—or, more likely, imagined loss—of your colleagues' respect and approval.

Actually, respect, approval, and admiration—even friendship and love—are given much more freely to people who are confident and secure in their personal finances, who are solvent and who've stopped debting, than they are to those who aren't and who haven't. This has been demonstrated repeatedly in my own life and in the lives of others who work the Back to the Black program.

There are many ways to avoid expenses and obtain non-debting money in the early stages of recovery. The list that follows contains some suggestions. This list, like all the others in the book, is meant partly to provide you with some practical ideas, but primarily to fire up your own imagination and to help you break through the barriers in your thinking. Keep in mind that most of these early measures are only temporary. As you progress, you'll be operating out of steadily increasingly income.

- Review the necessity of each expenditure, and do it with scrupulous honesty. If you don't absolutely need to make it, defer it till a later date.
- Cash a check or take money out of your savings account, even if it's the last money in there.
- Brown-bag your lunch to work instead of buying it out.
- Empty the container into which you toss your change. For most people, this gives them an immediate $20 to $200.
- Liquidate an asset such as a stock certificate or bond, even if you take a loss on it.
- Barter something. Offer to baby-sit your neighbors' child for one night if they'll baby-sit yours tonight. Exchange services—clerical work in your doctor's office for the ser-

vices you need from him. Your legal skills for someone else's carpentry skills. Your expertise in any area in exchange for someone else's that you need.

- Sell some personal possession, such as a piece of clothing, furniture, artwork, or set of silverware, that you don't really need or to which you're not deeply attached.
- Collect a debt owed to you, money you loaned to someone.
- Collect payment on an outstanding bill owed to you.
- Collect back salary or wages.
- Inform a client or customer that you can't front the cost of materials and bill them later. They must pay for the materials at the start.
- Cancel an order and reclaim your deposit.
- Go through the suits, jackets, pants, and dresses in your closet, and through your wallets and purses. This often turns up $10 to $100.
- Request a small cash gift, *not* a loan, from a relative.
- Ask your employer to give you the commission *already owed* to you for sales already made, or at least a portion of that, today.
- Stay home and watch television instead of going out to a movie.
- Take a bus instead of a cab.

Sit down and write out your own list. Let your imagination run free. You'll quickly discover that one idea triggers another. Don't limit yourself to the familiar and the obvious. Be as wild and improbable as you can. Remember, you're hurdling old mental barricades and breaking out into the open.

To your surprise, you'll find that in only ten or twenty minutes you will come up with many more ideas than you'd have thought possible at first. Some will be more desirable than others and not all will be equally feasible, especially if you really have been thinking in a wild and zany way. That's fine—the point is to get down as many as possible. Even if only half prove truly practical, the more you've listed, then the more real possibilities you've found.

Draw up this kind of list—and the other lists for which models are provided—as often as you need to. Even if you don't feel a need, it's a good idea to do one occasionally just to stimulate your imagination, to encourage your mind to keep thinking in innovative ways. The more you do them, the better and more creative you'll become at them.

8

A TOOL
NEARLY AS GOOD
AS THE WHEEL

We devoted the last chapter to a single idea—not debting, one day at a time—in order to stress its crucial importance. For the same reason, we're going to spend this chapter on a single tool. A tool is an implement or practical device you use to accomplish a job. In this case, the job is to achieve solvency.

The *Spending Record* is an enormously powerful tool, though its full value may not be apparent to you at first glance. It is so vital that, without it, most attempts to bring debting to a halt will end in futility. Like not debting one day at a time, the Spending Record is a key factor in recovery.

Clarity about your money is essential. You need to know where it's going before you can even begin to make effective changes. That may sound obvious, but it's not. Beyond the rent and a close guess on utilities, most people in debt can not tell you how much they spend each month, or on what.

An exaggeration?

How much did *you* spend last month?

How much did you spend on clothes? On newspapers, magazines? In coffee shops and on fast food? On cabs? On entertainment? On cosmetics? Laundry?

In most cases, the money comes in, the money goes out—

who knows where?—and there's never quite enough. This financial fog, this cloud of unknowing, is catastrophic. It leads almost inevitably to new debt. So long as you remain ignorant, you remain in the dark, blind and helpless. The Spending Record turns on the lights. It gives you knowledge. And that knowledge is power: Once you *know* what's happening, you can begin to work with it.

The Spending Record is *not* a budget. It is not a set of goals or guidelines. It is simply a record of the money you actually *do* spend. It allows you to see—possibly for the first time—where your money is going.

The Daily Record

You need a record of the cash you spent today. The daily record is not a plan; it's nothing more than a list of what you actually *did* spend, and on what.

All you need to do is jot down the amount, when you make an expenditure, and note what it was for. Some people keep a little spiral notebook in their purse or briefcase, others a piece of paper in their wallet. I carry a pen and a folded piece of paper in my shirt pocket.

Write down the day's date before you leave the house in the morning. Each time you spend cash during the day—whether to purchase something or to pay a bill—write down that expense. Note *how much* you spent, and *what* you spent it on.

For example:

TUESDAY, JULY 1

Newspaper	.50
Cab	6.75
Coffee shop	6.00
Lunch	10.00
Bus	1.50
Shaving cream, razors	11.61
Groceries	29.53

That's all there is to it. It couldn't be easier. On an average, it requires less than two minutes a day to accomplish.

Yet its effect is awesome. You'll never again put $40, $75, or $100 in your wallet and then wonder the next day, with bafflement and frustration, just where it all went. For the first time, you'll *know* where it went—precisely where. Keeping the record is a quantum leap toward gaining control over your money and your life.

Keep in mind the following points about the daily record:

1. It's a *daily* record, not a now-and-then record. It will do you no good to keep it on a hit-or-miss basis.
2. Record *each* and *every* expense—from a $75 sweater to a 50¢ pack of gum. The record is useless if it's incomplete.
3. Record the expense as soon as possible after making it. If you don't, you'll forget some.
4. Write down the amount to the *penny*.

"To the penny? That's ridiculous. That's nitpicking and make-work."

No, it's not.

Most debtors walk around in a fog about their money. The purpose of the record is to burn that fog away. Being exact maximizes your focus. Also, consistently rounding off—especially when several small expenditures are made each day—can result in underrecording expenses by as much as $150 a month, or $1,800 a year. That's a big chunk of money to be ignorant about.

So, one day at a time, keep the daily record. Write down the nature of the expense. Write down the exact amount. Make the entry as soon after the expense as you can. I usually step to the side after I've paid at the cash register or pause a moment when I get out into the street.

Noncash Expenses

When you pay for something by check, in effect you're paying cash. That's certainly part of your daily expenses—you spent that money today, regardless of how long it takes the recipient to cash the check. However, there's no point entering it on your record. That would only be a duplication of effort: The information in your checkbook is sufficient.

Be sure, though, to enter the information in your checkbook, and to do so immediately. Record the number of the check, the date, to whom it was payable, and what it was for. A notation that on July 1 you wrote a check for $95 to Neiman-Marcus is insufficient. What was the money spent on—household furnishings, clothes, recreational equipment? Without that information, you don't know where the money went.

Your checkbook ledger might look like this:

NUMBER	DATE	PAYEE	AMOUNT	BALANCE
456	7/1	Atwood Realty (rent)	$1,239.96	$1,832.12
457	7/1	New York Telephone Co.	96.71	1,735.41
458	7/1	Sloan's (groceries)	75.31	1,660.10
459	7/1	Ridgemark (shoes)	115.64	1,544.46
460	7/1	Hank's Garage (tune-up)	128.14	1,416.32

In my experience, as many as three-quarters of all debtors are so haphazard with their checkbook ledger that it's useless to them, that it only thickens the fog.

You may be like Lynn, an assistant network television producer, who used to practice what she later came to call "intuitive checking." She *never* entered her checks. Instead, she relied entirely on her "sense" of what was in her account—she also used to bounce thirty or forty checks a year and was $41,000 in debt when she began this program.

Or you may simply be the kind of person who's in a hurry

and sure you'll remember the information later. But then, tomorrow or next week, when you go to write a new check, you find you don't have the faintest recollection of what that missing check was for. Cash? A bill? Something you bought? Did you write it for $25, $50, $200? Confusion increases, clarity fades.

What about purchases you make on a credit card or a department store charge account? Do you record them on the daily record too? No. For a very simple reason—just for today, you're not going to make any. They're debts, remember? When you buy on credit, you incur a debt. And just for today, you're not going to do that.

The daily record, then, is simply a list of your cash expenses for the day, backed up by your checkbook entries. It's not complicated. It requires only a few moments of your time. Yet through it, the fog starts to lift, knowledge begins, and the power to reclaim your life comes.

The Weekly Record

The weekly record is a summary of your daily expenses over the course of one week. It tells you how much you spent that week and where your money went. (We're not talking about a week as it's usually conceived, one that begins on Monday and ends the following Sunday; here, we mean a week by calendar dates—for example, the period that begins July 1st and ends July 7th; it makes no difference whether July 1st happens to fall on a Wednesday or any other day.)

For simplicity's sake, divide the month into four one-week periods—with the final "week," of course, being seven to ten days long. For example:

- July 1–7 (first week)
- July 8–14 (second week)

- July 15–21 (third week)
- July 22–31 (fourth week)

Write the week-dates, as in the example that follows, at the top of a piece of paper. Then make a vertical list of the categories in which you spent money—for example: "Rent," "Groceries," "Clothes." Consult your daily records for that week. Add up each day's expenditures in a given category— "Groceries," for example—and enter the total for the week next to that category. Now do the same with the entries in your checkbook ledger.

Your weekly record might look like this:

JULY 1–7	
Rent	1,239.96
Groceries	139.66
Clothes	38.39
Entertainment	19.00
Laundry	15.50
Medical	81.00
Telephone	79.73
Transportation	29.56
TOTAL	$1,642.80

That's all there is to the weekly record. It usually takes only fifteen or twenty minutes to complete.

The Monthly Record

No, we haven't set off on an endless series of records. This is the last one. The monthly record is a summary of your weekly expenses for the month. It tells you exactly how much you spent that month, and on what. To keep it, all you have to do is add up your weekly expenses in each category to arrive at the month's totals. Most people incorporate their weekly records into their monthly record, combining them to make one form.

A simplified monthly record might look like this:

SPENDING RECORD FOR JULY

WEEK	1	2	3	4	TOTAL
Rent	$1,239.96				1,239.96
Food	139.66	116.88	129.60	150.90	537.04
Clothes	38.39	24.30	8.00		70.69
Entertainment	19.00		9.75	32.40	61.15
Gas & Electric	84.45				84.45
Laundry	15.50	5.60		29.00	50.10
Medical	81.00	20.13			101.13
Papers & Magazines	12.75	9.76	3.80	18.63	44.94
Telephone	79.73			1.25	80.98
Transportation	29.56	24.00	16.00	25.50	95.06
TOTALS	$1,740.00	$200.67	$167.15	$257.68	$2,365.50

The monthly Spending Record is a record of what you actually *are* spending. Its sole purpose is to let you know where your money is going. Now let's discuss it in more detail.

An Emerging Vision

You know what the Spending Record is, and you know how to keep it. Good. You have a vehicle. It'll get you where you want to go. But it's pretty crude, isn't it? Kind of like a Stanley Steamer, which was one of the first horseless carriages. The Stanley Steamer had wooden wheels and was powered by a kerosene-fired steam engine. We're going to turn that Stanley Steamer into a finely crafted, high-performance vehicle of immense power.

One of the primary functions of the Spending Record is to provide you with a revealing portrait of your life. It will teach you an incredible amount about how you *actually* live. In turn, those facts will tell you more about how you view yourself, your money, and your life in general than probably anything else ever has or will.

The key lies in the categories. The more precise they are, the more accurate a picture they give you. And the more accurate the picture, the better able you are to take control of your money and your life. Assume, for instance, that the monthly record in the preceding example is yours. You spent $537.04 for food. That's good to know, but it doesn't really tell you much. The category is too vague. Let's break it down into something more precise:

Fast Food/Diners
Groceries
Restaurants

"Fast Food/Diners" represents food out, the eating you do in places like pizza shops, delis, lunch counters, and coffee shops. "Groceries" covers the food you buy to cook and eat at home. The eating you do at restaurants also represents food, but it's more than that—it's also a pleasurable experience you give to yourself.

So instead of simply "Food—$537.04," let's say you have:

Fast Food/Diners 330.00
Groceries 207.04
Restaurants 0

What does this tell us? One, that you're probably not taking good nutritional care of yourself. Two, that you're wasting money; even a burger, fries, and a Coke aren't cheap these days. Three, that you've probably lost some of your capacity to enjoy food, since you're doing a lot of eating at diners. And four, that you're depriving yourself of pleasure. Going to a restaurant to sit in quiet, pleasant surroundings and eat a meal prepared and served to you by someone else is, for most people, a pleasurable experience.

The first and last of these points are probably the most significant. The pressure of debt usually results in a general deterioration of the quality of life, which often includes nutrition. This in itself can increase stress, diminish energy, and exaggerate already bleak emotions. And personal pleasure is one of the first areas in which debtors commonly try to cut back—the restaurants go, the symphonies go, the new clothes, the theater, books and records, vacations, dance and exercise classes. As these and similar pleasures disappear, life grows ever more grim until, at the extreme, you're living almost entirely for your creditors.

My own first Spending Record didn't even *contain* a category for entertainment. My friend Ed pointed out its absence.

"The first thing you have to do," he said, "is start spending money on yourself."

That statement was nearly incomprehensible to me then.

Nor did I have a category for personal care—toothpaste, antiperspirants, shoe polish, and such. I'd lumped those under "Food," since that included everything I bought at the supermarket.

"And not just haircuts and toothpaste," Ed said, "but stuff like massages, though some people prefer to put that under the 'Health' category. I think of it as personal care myself."

"Massages?"

"Or yoga classes," he said, "scuba diving, whatever. It's up to you. But one thing's certain—if you don't learn how to give to yourself and start enjoying life again, you're never going to get out of this."

The Spending Record can tell you a lot.

Categories

Most people break their spending into twenty-five to thirty-five categories. Avoid extremes at either end. Too few, and you're still enveloped in fog. Too many, and you over-complicate the record. Creating a Spending Record is a process. You'll alter it as your awareness grows and as change occurs in your life. I don't even recollect what version I'm on these days.

Draw up an initial record immediately. Make half a dozen photocopies to use over the next few months. Or create and keep the record on a software program. As ideas for change occur, jot yourself a note and put it in a file. Take this file out at intervals of six months or so and revise your record; the point is to keep it accurate and functional but not to drive yourself nuts with constant change.

The only hard-and-fast rule about categories is to be precise. If you have an especially large expense, such as therapy, it's best to make that a separate category rather than to subsume it under your "Medical" category. If you're a passionate skier and spend a lot on equipment, clothes, lessons, travel, and resorts, it's best to make "Skiing" a separate category. If you were to put those expenses variously under, say, "Clothes," "Recreation," and "Travel," you wouldn't really know how much you actually spend on skiing.

The following is a list of the most common categories. Some won't apply to you, and you'll probably need a few that don't appear here.

- Alimony
- Books
- Cabs/Limousines
- Car (gasoline, tires, insurance, maintenance, and repair)
- Charitable Contributions
- Child Support

- Children's Expenses
- Clothes
- Cosmetics
- Diners/Fast Food
- Dry Cleaning
- Education
- Entertainment (movies, theater, concerts, galleries, day excursions, circus, fair, video arcade)
- Entertainment Others (this indicates that you took a date or friend out and paid for him or her)
- Gas/Electricity
- Gifts
- Groceries
- Haircuts/Beauty Salon
- Health Club
- Hobby
- Home Equipment (television, radio, dishes, pots and pans, appliances, tools)
- Home Furnishings (tables, chairs, beds, rugs, drapes)
- Home Heating
- Home Repair/Maintenance (painting, plumbing, wiring, storm windows, heating system, roofing, insurance, landscaping)
- Home Supplies (paper towels, sponges, dish and laundry soap, steel-wool pads, toilet paper, scouring powder, floor wax, string, tape)
- House Cleaning
- Income Taxes (if you're self-employed and they're not deducted from salary, or if they're assessed beyond amount withheld)
- Investments
- Laundry
- Legal Expenses
- Life Insurance
- Magazines/Newspapers

- Medical (doctors, prescriptions, glasses, medicine-chest supplies)
- Medical Insurance
- Personal Care (shampoo, nail scissors, soap, razors and blades, toothbrushes, hairbrushes, combs, perfume or cologne)
- Personal Growth (lectures, seminars, special training or courses)
- Pet
- Professional Dues
- Property Taxes
- Public Transportation (buses, subways, trains, ferries)
- Rent/Mortgage
- Restaurants
- Restaurants Others (paying for someone else's dinner)
- Sport
- Telephone
- Therapy
- Tips/Gratuities
- Tuition
- Union Dues
- Vacation/Travel
- Vitamins
- Miscellaneous (any little oddity that doesn't fit into the other categories; however, if the total here is consistently over $20, you probably need a new category or two)

Use or modify any of these categories for your own record, and add any not mentioned here that you specifically need. Rank your categories in the way that seems easiest for you. Some people place the obvious ones like "Rent" and "Groceries" at the top, then list the others in alphabetical order.

The Spending Record

Most people can draw up an initial Spending Record in an hour or two. That's a small investment in exchange for so powerful a tool. Below is what a typical record might look like.

WEEK	1	2	3	4	Total
Rent					
Groceries					
Books					
Buses/Subways					
Cabs					
Car					
Child Support					
Cigarettes					
Clothes					
Diners/Fast Food					
Electricity					
Entertainment					
Gifts					
House Equipment					
House Supplies					
Laundry					
Magazines/Papers					
Medical					
Miscellaneous					
Personal Care					
Taxes					
Telephone					
TOTALS:					

SPENDING RECORD
MONTH OF _____ 20____

Resistance

Initial reaction to the Spending Record breaks pretty consistently into three camps: About a third respond with immediate enthusiasm and plunge right into it; another third are lukewarm, even reluctant, but are willing to give it a try; and the final third are either angry or frightened and don't want anything to do with it.

Anger is usually a form of denial. The sheer fact of keeping a Spending Record carries with it an implied admission that you're in trouble with debt. Refusing to keep it serves your denial: "You may have a problem, but *I* don't."

So off you go, back into the wild blue yonder of credit and debt until, finally, it gets so bad you no longer have a choice. Until your finances are utterly wrecked and the creditors are howling at your door. Danny, the welder who's still out there debting and growing more desperate every month, was indignant when I suggested that he keep a record.

Fear is also usually nothing more than a form of denial: If you don't look at it, it's not there, or maybe it will simply go away. As long as it's not down in black and white, you can tell yourself it's not as bad as you're afraid it might be.

Noreen, the children's book editor who ran from this program after her first encounter with it, stopped debting immediately after she returned, and willingly participated in meetings, but couldn't bring herself to begin keeping a record. "I don't *know* what I'm afraid of," she said. "All I know is that my hands start to sweat and I want to run and hide under the bed whenever I think about it."

Despite her fear, she finally did take the plunge in her third month—and her record revealed to her that her basic expenses were actually somewhat *less* than her net income.

The irony is that most people, like Noreen, discover their situation is not as bad as they had feared; fear served only to deny them the relief that finally came with that discovery.

. . .

The Spending Record is a powerful tool. It's also vital. Without it, you're unlikely to liberate yourself from debt. I've never known anyone who did. I have known several who tried and failed. Keeping the record is an important step in your recovery. Begin your daily record tomorrow. This coming weekend, take the time to create a monthly Spending Record for yourself. If you're going to keep the record by hand, make half a dozen photocopies so you have a sufficient supply. The sooner you begin to work the record, the sooner it will begin to work for you; and you'll be astounded by how much it can do for you.

9

GETTING STRONGER

You've mastered two fundamental parts of this program: One day at a time you don't debt, and you're keeping the Spending Record. This in itself has already carried you a good distance toward the goal of liberating yourself from debt and going on to live in prosperity. You're much stronger now than you were when you first opened this book. You're taking control of your life. Your vision is becoming clearer. In this chapter we're going to increase that strength and sharpen that vision.

The Devil You Know

Many people, when they begin the Back to the Black program, don't even know what their total debt is or all the creditors they owe. This is crippling ignorance.

The devil you know is much better than the devil you don't. It's time now to make a complete list of your debts and creditors. Some people panic at this point, as if committing this information to paper will breathe life into a dormant monster. If you're one of these, realize that there is *nothing* in this action that will hurt you or worsen your situation.

These debts already exist. If you keep trying to reject them from your consciousness, you'll only open yourself to increasing pressure and difficulty.

You have to know *what* you're working with before you can work with it. We don't give a damn about repayment here. All we want is a clear and complete list.

To their amazement, many people discover they actually owe *less* than they had feared. Lynn, the television producer who once practiced "intuitive checking," was originally as ignorant of her real debt as she was of her checking account balance. She guessed that her debt was about $115,000. When she drew up a list she found that the true total was $62,000! Her mind had magnified it over the years to nearly twice its actual amount. Lynn's case is extreme, but the fact remains: People often discover they owe less than they thought.

Make your debt list on a pad of paper. Place the name of the creditor on the left, the amount you owe on the right. It's easier to be thorough if you approach this list in terms of categories. List *every* debt, whether it's $1 or $100,000. We want a complete picture. Remember, for our purposes a secured loan is *not* a debt. So place only unsecured loans on this list.

Institutional Loans These are loans from banks or other lending institutions, usually granted on the basis of your signature alone. The reason you gave to obtain the loan—home improvement, working capital, vacation—is irrelevant here; the point is that if it is an unsecured loan, it is a debt.

If you've dealt with two or more institutions, list each institution separately. If you've taken out more than one loan from a given institution, make a separate entry for each loan. For example:

AMALGAMATED BANK

June $2,500

HOUSEHOLD FINANCE CO.

March $2,900
May $5,500

Checking Overdraft This is known by many names—Checking Plus, Cash Reserve Checking, and the like. It is an overdraft privilege, a personal credit line that allows you to write checks for more money than you have in your account. The bank covers them by placing its own money at your disposal up to a prearranged amount, usually $2,000 to $10,000. This is an automatic loan. It is an unsecured debt; you have borrowed money from the bank and they have no collateral from you.

Write down the amount you currently owe your bank under this system.

Credit Cards Here we're concerned with the total amount you owe on a given credit card. Separate these card by card: American Express, Diners Club, and so on.

If you hold several cards under the same generic name—Visa or MasterCard, for example—but issued from different sources, then make a separate entry for each source. For example:

Visa (Chase) $5,000
Visa (Citibank) $3,100
Visa (Barclays) $2,350

Department Stores List each department store or retail store at which you have a charge account, and the outstanding balance on each account.

Educational Loans The most common sources for these are the federal government, a private bank, the school you attended, and your state's higher education authority. Each loan should be listed separately.

Personal Loans These are loans taken from relatives and friends. Here you can add together all the different loans from the same individual and enter the total amount you owe to that person. For example, if you borrowed $2,000 from your father two years ago, another $2,500 last year, and $1,000 this year, make a single entry:

Father $5,500

But do make a separate entry for each individual.

Salary Advances List the amount of salary, wages, or commissions advanced to you by your employer. If you've received advances from more than one employer, list each separately.

Services Rendered List each person or organization from whom you've received a service for which there's a balance outstanding. These might include your doctor, dentist, accountant, architect, agent, TV repairman, carpenter, electrician, plumber, car mechanic, garbage service, lawn maintenance service, or pool service.

Rent Enter the amount of back rent you owe.

Utilities List any past-due bills you owe for telephone, gas, electric, water, or sewer service.

Income Taxes Separately, list any back taxes you owe the IRS, state, county, or city. Include penalties and interest in the total amount you owe to each agency.

Property Taxes Enter any back property taxes you owe.

Others If you are in debt to creditors not included in the above, list each of them too.

Have you completed this list? Good. Add up the total.

Now sit back in your chair and relax. Take a couple of slow, deep breaths. Close your eyes. Remind yourself that it's not Armageddon. You owe some money, that's all. The missiles won't be launched, blood isn't running in the streets. Get grounded in today, in right now, this very moment. Right now, today, you are perfectly all right. You have everything you need. Here is an important point to remember about the amount of your total debt:

The Figure Is Not Relevant.

No matter what the figure is, *this* is how much you really owe——more than some, less than others. What is significant is not how big or how small your total debt is, but the destructive impact continuing debt and continued debting have upon your life. The man or woman who's $1,000 in debt and falling in deeper each month experiences just as much pain as the one who's $20,000 or $200,000 in debt and falling in deeper each month. When there's not enough money the stress is the same, no matter what the numbers are. So the amount you owe, whatever that may be, is irrelevant as far as your recovery is concerned. What is relevant is this program. If you follow its principles you will liberate yourself from debt, no matter how much you owe.

To remind you that you're not alone and that thousands have already broken the trail before you, here's what my own list looked like when I began, back in 1984:

Chemical Bank	$17,500
American Express	256
Visa (Citibank)	1,493
Visa (Chemical Bank)	502
MasterCard	364
Authors Guild	2,500
Attorney	1,500

```
Book Packager  . . . . . . . . . . . . . . .15,000
Father  . . . . . . . . . . . . . . . . . . . . . .9,000
Bob  . . . . . . . . . . . . . . . . . . . . . . . . .500
Matt . . . . . . . . . . . . . . . . . . . . . . . . .500
```
Total: $49,115

I owed more than some, less than others.

In identifying and adding up your debts, you've taken another major step toward total freedom from debt: You know what you're working with now. This list should be a source of self-esteem for you. It was an act of courage to make it.

The Plastic, of Course

You probably feared that this was coming. Indeed it was, and here it is: Keeping a credit card in your wallet is like carrying around a hand grenade with a loose pin—sooner or later, it's going to go off.

"But . . . !"

"But . . . !"

"But . . . !"

Right. Everyone says that.

There is only one thing you can do with a credit card—debt. That's a simple fact, but few are willing to face it at first. Most come up with several reasons why they *need* a credit card. The most common are:

- To rent a car
- To avoid carrying cash
- For identification
- To make purchases over the telephone
- For business reasons
- In case of emergencies
- Because it makes life easier

Let's examine these, beginning with the broadest one.

"It Makes Life Easier."

Yes, it does. Without a credit card, you'll sometimes have to think a bit, occasionally you'll have to make alternate arrangements, and now and then you'll be inconvenienced. That's definitely true.

But the time you might spend and the inconvenience you might undergo are relatively minor. Despite what you may think, it's fairly easy to live in this society without a credit card. Nearly everyone who follows this program is doing so right now, and has been for years. Yet initial resistance to the idea is nearly universal, even among people who have clearly brutalized themselves with credit cards.

Catherine, the editor who'd been on the verge of suicide, agonized over the issue for two weeks. She owed more than $16,000 on her various cards, but still she didn't want to give them up. She asked me to meet her, to give her moral support. We sat down in a booth in a diner. She'd brought all her cards. She lined them up on the table in three rows. There were twelve of them: two MasterCards, three Visas, a gold American Express, a Carte Blanche, a B. Altman's, a Bloomingdale's, a Macy's, an American Airlines, and a Mobil Oil. She stared at them.

"I don't know if I can do this," she said in a cracking voice.

She took a scissors from her purse. Her hands shook. One by one, she cut the cards in half, wincing as each one fell. In the end, there remained only the American Express gold card.

"Please," she said, in almost a whimper. "Please, not this one too. This is my *dignity*."

That was horrifying—that a human being had been so eroded by her debts that the only place she could find her dignity, her sense of worth, was in a piece of plastic. Giving it to a clerk, she *was* somebody.

She cut that one too, then slumped back and stared into her lap. "I feel sick," she said. "I feel lost and all alone."

Today, Catherine is thriving. More and more, she's finding her dignity *within* herself. She can scarcely comprehend the person she was back then, that years of mounting debt had made of her.

"But *I'm* different," you might say. "*I* don't have anywhere near twelve cards, and I don't owe them $16,000 either."

Neither did a lot of others when they began this program. The numbers don't make any difference. It's the instant access to debt we're talking about.

Russ, a university professor, has been working this program for two years. He'd never had more than one credit card in his life, and two years ago he owed only $600 on it. It wasn't a problem for him, he claimed, and he had no intention of giving it up. Yet despite his determination, he used the card repeatedly over the next six months—when he was caught short, to cheer himself up, and sometimes just on impulse. He had sworn to pay for each new purchase in full when the bill arrived, but he never had quite enough to spare, and he continued to debt, and the total he owed rose each month.

Finally, in frustrated anger, he surrendered, and destroyed the card. "It was neither the deprivation nor the defeat I thought it would be," he said later. "Actually, it was a great relief. I ended up feeling lighter and happier."

A credit card is a hand grenade. It is instant debt.

"Wait a minute," you might say (as many have), "I can see the point with credit cards, but what about my American Express? *That's* not a credit card. You can't pay it off in installments. The full amount is due each month. It's no different from your telephone."

You're happy. You've found an out. You get to keep your American Express card. It's true—the American Express card is not a credit card. But it works just as well as one, and you can get just as far into debt with it—as many people in recovery know very well.

In actual practice, you can be a month late on your payment to American Express. And two months late, or even three, before they'll threaten to revoke your card. And some people have been able to negotiate a partial-payment arrangement with American Express.

But most importantly, there is this: You can't take your telephone into The Wiz and charge a $500 television set on it. You can't take your telephone to your travel agent and charge tickets to Paris on it. But you can do that, and a hell of a lot more, with an American Express card. So, for practical purposes, an American Express card is no different from a Visa card. Neither are department store charge accounts. The only thing you can do with them is debt. Therefore . . .

Right. Take all your plastic, and cut it up. If you don't have the cards, you can't use them. Destroying them is the most important step, but you should also notify the supplier that you wish to cancel the account. This completes the act and prevents any possible future problem with the account.

Most suppliers will try to talk you out of canceling, which is quite natural; after all, they're making 15 to 24 percent annual interest on your balance. Remain friendly and polite, but be firm. If you wish, you can tell them simply that you prefer to pay by cash from here on, but you don't have to give them any explanation at all.

"I Need a Credit Card in Order to Rent a Car."

Nearly everyone who lives in a city and doesn't own a car cites this one first. It's as if the only possibility of exit or mobility is by a car rented on a credit card.

When Glen, the actor, insisted he couldn't possibly give up his credit card, his reason was this: A year or two from now he might land a big role in a film or television series. He'd have to go out to Los Angeles. That city is a car city. You can't get around there without one. He'd have to rent a car, and to do that he would need a credit card.

This was incredible. Here was a man $15,000 in debt, whose career was at a stall point (largely because of the emotional state his debting had caused), who was driving a limousine part time and working the night shift twice a week as a legal proofreader, who was barely covering his minimal expenses and didn't know how he was going to make his rent from month to month, worrying about his need to rent a car two years from now! The pressure of debt truly distorts our vision. And denial can be formidable.

To set the record straight: No matter what you've been told and despite your contrary convictions, you *can* rent a car without a credit card. In fact, more companies permit this than do not. You have to apply for the privilege in advance. To qualify, you need in most cases to have worked for the same employer for a year or more, to have lived at the same address for a year or more, and to have a checking account, a savings account, and a telephone listed in your name at the address that appears on your driver's license. You'll have to leave a cash deposit when you rent the car. The amount varies from company to company and according to geography and the type of car you're renting. One company, for example, requires either $250 or 150 percent of the estimated rental fee, whichever is greater. If renting a car is a real concern to you, canvass your area to find out what is possible.

If no agency within range of you has the provision we've just described—which is unlikely—and you absolutely must have a car—then find another way to get one, such as borrowing or renting a friend's. This is a good time to use your growing list-making abilities. Sit down with a pad of paper. Across the top, write: Ways I Can Gain Access to a Car Without Using a Credit Card. Break down the old barricades in your thinking. Unleash your imagination and let it run free.

"I Need a Credit Card for Identification."

You need identification primarily for cashing checks or paying for purchases by check. But most check cashing is done at your own bank or one of its branches, where you're known to the tellers or can use an ATM card or other non-credit-card identification. The same is true when you cash a check with a local merchant or a friend. You don't need a credit card in these situations. And when you wish to buy something from a large department store or a retailer who's unfamiliar with you, many alternate kinds of identification are perfectly acceptable. People who work this program have successfully used all of the following:

- Driver's license
- ATM card
- Debit card
- Passport
- Pistol permit
- Blue Cross/Blue Shield card
- Various company photo IDs
- Official badge
- Utility bill with name and address
- Notarized birth certificate
- Automobile registration
- Club membership card
- Various civil service IDs
- Union identification card
- Alien registration card
- Active military ID
- Retired military ID

Of these, a driver's license is the most common and useful. But the range of possibilities is wide. In one case, a man used a traffic ticket he'd been issued that morning. In another, an author who was buying books took down one of her own novels from the shelf and showed her photo on the back to the clerk.

You don't need a credit card for identification.

"I Don't Want to Carry Cash."

Many people aren't comfortable putting a couple of hundred dollars in their wallet. They're afraid of robbery or loss, they think. Actually, the discomfort stems largely from the fact that the act is utterly alien to them. Robbery and loss of wallet aren't as common as you think. How many times have you or any of your close friends been robbed? How many times have you lost your wallet? I was robbed once, in 1969. I lost my wallet three times, first in 1960, again in 1972, and the last time in 1991.

I'm not suggesting that you carry around thousands of dollars with brazen unconcern. Or even that you carry a large amount of cash every day. Just that you experiment a little and determine where your own comfort zone is. Mine, on a day I intend to go shopping with cash, is about $500. Most other days I don't need more than $100 or so.

If you want to make a truly large purchase, in the range of several hundred dollars or more, then make it with a check. Some people who want or need a daily amount larger than they're comfortable with carry traveler's checks.

"I Can't Make Telephone Purchases Without One."

In most cases, you can. You can order the goods COD or with a debit card or ask the seller to place them on hold for you and send a check off that same afternoon. When none of these is possible, find another source for the goods you want.

"I Need One for Business Reasons."

This usually translates to taking a client to lunch. You can pay in cash when you do that. You can use a debit card. You can use a company card, which is billable directly to the company. You can make special arrangements.

Martha, who has her own advertising agency, takes most of her clients to one of three restaurants where she has an arrangement. When the check is presented, she simply signs it. Later in the afternoon, back in her office, she sends her own check over to the restaurant by messenger or drops it off on her way home.

Airline and hotel reservations generally can be made in advance by sending a deposit check and can usually be paid for at the end of your stay by debit card, personal check, or traveler's check. You can eliminate potential problems by determining what's necessary ahead of time.

"I Need One for Emergencies."

What emergencies?

Nuclear attack? Riot and civil disorder?

This one comes up frequently. But when asked, no one can define just what they mean by it. *Something* might happen. Perhaps you'll wake up naked, penniless, hungry, all alone, and out in the elements—with only your trusty credit card clutched in your hand to save you. Happens all the time.

I've never had a single emergency in which a credit card could have done any more for me than cash did, or a check or telephone call. What most people mean when they say "I need a credit card for emergencies" is this: *I need a credit card in case I run out of money*. But the only thing you can do with that credit card is debt. And it's your previous debting that has caused this fear of running out of money.

The day you stop debting is the day you will begin to bring more money into your life. Then and only then will there be enough, and only then will the fear of running out begin to leave you. You can not free yourself from debt by borrowing more money.

A Cautious Exception

Clearly, then, it is very much in your self-interest to get rid of your credit cards. In fact, it's nearly essential. But am I telling you that no one who kept a credit card ever succeeded at this program? I'm tempted to say yes—because I've seen so many try it and fail. But the answer is no. A few have, though I grant this reluctantly for fear you'll seize upon it as permission.

Lois, for example, is a concert pianist. She is frequently on tour. To simplify her many necessary transactions, and to assist in record keeping, she uses an American Express card when she has to travel.

So does Shep, an electronics engineer whose business takes him across the United States and to Europe.

But both these people have embarked on a strong recovery program, and both are careful and quite conscious of the way they use the card. I'm opposed to maintaining a card in nearly every case; no matter how you look at it, it is instant access to debt. But if you're rock sure of your personal discipline and have an *unequivocal* need for a credit card, then do this:

1. Keep the card in a drawer. Take it out only on the day you need it.
2. Know *exactly* what you're going to use it for before you put it in your wallet.
3. Use it for nothing but your intended purpose.
4. Return the card to its drawer as soon as you're back home.
5. Immediately write a check to the name of the card in the amount you charged, then deduct that amount from your checking account balance.

This last step is essential. It is consistent with the principle and practice of not debting; you spent that money today, it is no longer available to you. Deducting it immediately also leaves you with a true and accurate balance, a figure that represents the actual amount of money you have left to spend. If you continued to include in your balance the amount you already spent by using the card, you would cloud the picture and give yourself a false impression; your balance would tell you that you have more left than you really do.

Also, by writing the check and making the deduction at once, you'll never be caught off guard when the bill comes in. You won't have to say, "Oh God, another $300 I forgot about. Where am I going to get the money?" You've already paid this bill. All you have to do is place the check you wrote out on the day you used the card into the return envelope and mail it. Even better, mail the check the same day you write it, without waiting for the bill, or go online if you bank online and send payment out immediately.

Some people prepay their account, establishing a credit balance. (*No* issuer will refuse a prepayment.) This is especially useful when you're planning a trip and know you'll be using the card often. All you need do is maintain a running balance, deducting the day's charges at the end of the day.

It is never absolutely necessary, and only rarely advisable, to retain a credit card. I hope you don't. But if you do, then at the first misuse of it, the first debting, you have no choice but to destroy it and cancel your account if you truly wish to free yourself from debt. You've already made good progress toward putting your life back together; it doesn't make sense to blow yourself up again.

The Company Card

If you carry a company-sponsored card and are required to use it when doing business for the company, to be reimbursed later, you need to be very careful. Many people damage themselves and their relationship with the company in this situation, using the card for personal expenses or spending the reimbursement check on something else, telling themselves it's just this one time and that they'll straighten everything out in a month or two. But they don't, and the situation can go bad quickly, with the issuer of the card complaining to the company about nonpayment, and the company coming down on the employee. If you must use a company card, file for expenses beforehand if the company permits that and prepay the card, or talk over the problem with someone from your human resources department or employee assistance program.

The Debit Card

The debit card is an ideal solution for many people recovering from debt who are reluctant to carry substantial cash or occasionally want the same convenience a credit card offers. Most debit cards are linked with Visa or MasterCard and can be used anywhere a credit card can—shopping, eating out, air travel, and all the rest. But there's an important difference. The debit card is *not* a credit card. It carries no credit line. No money is ever advanced to you. You are never sent a bill.

Paying with a debit card is pretty much like paying with a check. As soon as the merchant's voucher reaches your bank (often instantaneously), the amount is deducted from your account. The transaction appears on your monthly statement, just as if you had written a check. Unlike a check, however, which can be written even if there are no funds in the bank and which will bounce unless covered in time, a debit card will be refused if there are insufficient funds available.

Debit cards were exotic and not widely available when I first wrote this book. To receive one, you had to open a checking account/money-market account with a sizeable initial deposit, often $10,000. That has changed dramatically. Now there are more than 100 million debit cards in circulation and they are nearly as easy to obtain as an ATM card.

One caveat about debit cards: If compulsive or chronic shopping is part of your history, you probably don't want to carry one on a daily basis and might not even want one at all. The card is easy to use and, being plastic, buying something with it doesn't seem for some people to be spending real money. It's only when their bank statement arrives or, worse, a check bounces that they realize what they have done with it. When you use a debit card, deduct the amount of your transaction immediately from your checking balance, since you just spent that money and no longer have it.

No Wild Promises

When an angry or demanding creditor confronts you, there's a powerful impulse to promise him practically anything to take the pressure off. That's natural. It's an unpleasant, sometimes excruciating event.

"Where's the money?"

"What are you, some kind of deadbeat?"

"Pay up. Now."

"I'm sick of your excuses."

"Where the hell is the rent?"

"You gave me the same song and dance last month."

"We're going to shut off your service."

"We're turning you over to a collection agency."

"We're taking you to court."

"We'll garnish your salary."

This kind of stuff can make you sick to your stomach. You're guilty, you're ashamed. You're enraged, panicky, helpless, and crazy. You'll promise them anything to make them stop, to make them leave you alone.

So you do. You tell them you'll send a check tomorrow, you'll give them $300 a month, you'll pay the whole thing off next week. And for the moment, the pressure's gone. But then the payment date falls due and you can't fulfill your promise, and everything goes from bad to worse. Your creditor feels you've lied to him once again. He becomes even angrier, even more threatening. Desperate, you make new promises, and when you can't keep those, everything goes from worse to horrible.

From Here On, Do Not Make a Single Promise to a Creditor Unless You Are Absolutely Sure You Can Keep It.

Not one. No matter how pressured or panicky you feel. If you promise a creditor something, then fail to keep that promise, you will inevitably only worsen your situation.

Thanks, but No Thanks

An enabler is someone who makes it easier for you to keep debting—usually a relative or friend, sometimes a business associate. Most often, an enabler is well meaning. She cares about you. She wants to help you out of a tight spot. So she lends you money. But all that loan really does is get you deeper into debt.

My own enabler was Bob; we had been close friends for many years, had celebrated triumphs together, and had stood by each other in times of anguish. At one point, it seemed to both of us that a series of difficult events in my life—ranging from a painful divorce to illness and a couple of professional setbacks—had combined to cause a temporary financial crisis, and that what I had to do was to borrow more in order to get through. Neither of us recognized then that the reverse was true, that the crisis was in fact the inevitable result of my increasing debting. Surely, we both thought, The Big Fix would arrive momentarily, and then everything would be all right. It was Bob who backed up my major loans, it was Bob who sent me personal checks, it was Bob, my very good friend, who said to me over long-distance telephone: "I won't let you go under."

And he did not, and I will always be deeply grateful.

But I went even deeper into debt.

When I finally came to understand what was happening and brought my debting to a halt, hope began to grow in me, but I was still fearful and filled with doubt. Bob sent me a final check, for $1,000. "Just in case something goes wrong," he said. "You've got to have *something*. Cash it when you need it."

I kept that check in a desk drawer for six weeks. Then I tore it up. The fear was still there, I wanted to hang on to the money, but I knew that I needed to commit, that I needed to say: *I will not debt, no matter what happens.* Destroying that check was a crucial step, a milestone in my recovery. Bob acted solely out of abiding friendship and a genuine desire to help. Nevertheless, his generosity only worsened my situation in the end. Each new loan I took simply put me deeper into debt and forestalled, for a little while longer, my inevitable bottoming out.

Sometimes there's a darker side to enablers: Consciously or subconsciously, they may be motivated by a desire to keep you incapable and dependent on them, or under their control. This occasionally comes into play between parents and an adult child, when the parents use loans to keep the grown child in a subservient position or to avoid letting go.

Chuck, a securities analyst, had debted most of his life. When his daughter was born, he was desperately pressed for money. His parents, who'd always enabled him, gave him a lump $30,000 as an open-ended loan. Over the next three

years they insisted more and more upon a say in his life, in
everything from the way he furnished his apartment to his
choice of vacation spots and even in the naming of his second child. If he tried to assert himself, they would appear
hurt, tell him they were only trying to help, and then make
some subtle reference to the loan. It wasn't until he stopped
debting and began to execute a repayment plan that he
began to feel entitled to his own life again.

Regardless of the enabler's motivation—even if it's
purely loving and selfless—his act of enabling only damages
you, only makes it easier for you to continue to debt.

So what do you do?

Thank your enabler for his concern and his desire to help.
Tell him that you're grateful for the help he's already given
you and that the best way you can demonstrate your gratitude is to pay him back, in full, as soon as you can; and point
out that the day will come much sooner if you don't borrow
any more from him.

If the relationship is close and well intentioned, you may
choose to be candid and tell your enabler about the recovery
program you've undertaken. When the enabler truly cares
for you, he nearly always understands and responds with
warmth and support. If you're not close or if you have
doubts, you might simply say that for reasons of bookkeeping or to simplify your responsibilities, you prefer to take no
additional loans. There is no "better" way in this, simply the
way with which you're most comfortable. But however you
do it, do it. Tell your enabler, "Thanks, but no thanks."

10

THE SPENDING PLAN

Once again we're going to devote a full chapter to a single tool—the Spending Plan. This tool will help you match your income to your needs, exercise clear options, and make informed choices about your money. It will bring into focus areas that need your attention and will enable you to take increasing control of your finances.

Bye-Bye Budget

The Spending Plan is *not* a budget. The word *budget* derives from the Old French *bougette,* the diminutive form of *bouge*—leather bag—and means a small purse. You can't carry much in a small purse. A sense of insufficiency and restriction is inherent in the word, a sense of not having enough. A budget confines you to a dark little room while everyone else is outside playing in the sunlight. It's no wonder that most people are depressed by budgets and don't stay with them very long.

A plan, on the other hand, is a detailed scheme, a method worked out beforehand to accomplish a goal. A general doesn't budget a victory, he *plans* a victory. A lover doesn't budget a romantic night, she *plans* a romantic night. The distinction is important. There's a world of psychological difference between a plan and a budget.

Ask yourself: "How do I plan to spend my money this weekend?"

Now ask: "How am I going to budget my money this weekend?"

It's not the same.

Budgets constrain and limit you. Plans give you choices and options. Budgets are fixed. Plans are flexible. Budgets lead to penny-pinching and deprivation. Plans encourage action and increase.

The Spending Plan is not an absolute. It is merely a set of guidelines to point you in the direction you wish to go. It's important, also, to understand that it's a thing of the moment. As you continue to work this program, your money will steadily increase and you'll revise your plan accordingly. In time, your expanding options will include what are usually called "luxury problems." Do I want a blazer, some shirts, and slacks or do I prefer a formal suit? Should I buy a video camera or new speakers? Do I wish to spend the money flying to Spain or renting a cabin in the Adirondacks? Everyone who works this program encounters such questions sooner or later.

The easiest way to create a Spending Plan form is to expand upon the form you're now using for your Spending Record. Work on your software program or get out a blank copy of your record to use as a model. If you're working on paper, draw up a new form on a separate sheet, altering the old one in this fashion:

1. Change the name of the last vertical column on the right from "Total" to "Actual."
2. Add a new vertical column to the right of that one and give it the heading "Plan."
3. Add a final vertical column to the right of the "Plan"

SPENDING RECORD
MONTH OF _____ 20____

WEEK	1	2	3	4	ACTUAL	PLAN	+ or –
Rent						1,240	
Groceries						210	
Books						30	
Buses/Subways						45	
Cabs						70	
Child Support						300	
Clothes						105	
Contributions						30	
Debt Repayment						165	
Diners/Fast Food						120	
Electricity						70	
Entertainment						65	
House Equipment						40	
House Furnishings						80	
House Supplies						30	
Laundry						30	
Magazines/Papers						40	
Medical						85	
Medical Insurance						165	
Miscellaneous						20	
Personal Care						65	
Restaurants						85	
Telephone						70	
TOTALS						$3,160	

column and mark this one "+ or −," which indicates plus or minus.

An example is on page 130. For the moment, ignore the figures that are entered in the "Plan" column. They're intended to serve as reference points for later topics in this chapter. When you draw up your own form, of course, the "Plan" column will be empty, like the others.

Putting It to Work

The primary purpose of the Spending Plan is to help you plan your expenses for the coming month. But before this can be done, it's necessary to know your *net* monthly income. That's the total you actually receive, in hand, after all deductions are removed. Be sure to include *all* your net income, regardless of its source. For those people who work at a fixed salary, the amount will be more or less constant (a promotion, bonus, job change, or other factors could alter it). For others, such as self-employed professionals, there might be significant differences month to month. To simplify, let's say that you're working with a net income of $3,100.

Formulate your Spending Plan early, preferably on the first day of the month (you need to wait till then because you're going to use last month's Spending Record to help you), but definitely no later than the second or third day.

Clear your desk. Place a blank copy of the Spending Plan before you and write the name of the month that is just beginning on the top. Now get out last month's Spending Record, which lists the totals that you *actually* did spend last month in each of your categories. These amounts are your starting point.

Think about each figure, one category at a time. Does it seem like you spent too much here, or maybe not enough? Let's use "Cabs" as an example. Assume that you spent $95 on cabs last month. Does that strike you as excessive, just right, or insufficient? Only you can decide. Let's say it seems high. So you decide you can cut your cab expenses down to $70 (the amount listed in the preceding example), without feeling that you're stinting yourself too much. Enter $70 in the cab category of the vertical "Plan" column in your Spending Record (which, in this new form, is both a plan and a record).

Go through each of your categories in a similar manner, deciding how much you want to spend in them this month—less than you did last month, more than you did, or about the same.

Let's say you've done that, and the result is the Spending Plan we've given as an example. Looking at it, you'll note that your planned expenditures come out pretty close to your $3,100 net income. This example isn't a stacked deck—in most cases, the entries on a first Spending Plan total an amount that's surprisingly close to the money actually available. In this case, you're only $60 over.

Not bad—but it's still too much, unless you want to sell something, put in overtime, or find some other way to get your net income up to $3,160 or more for the month. Or you could cut expenses by $60. You'll have to do one or the other: Otherwise, if you lived up to the letter of your plan, you would debt. You can't make $3,100 and spend $3,160 without debting. In our model plan, the places to cut would be in the categories of telephone, contributions, house furnishings, or debt repayment. (For now, keep debt repayment to the barest minimum; we'll discuss that subject in detail in Chapters 16 through 18.) Eating more at home and less at diners and fast-food places would cut expenses too.

The categories you should *not* trim are those that contribute to your daily sense of well-being and pleasure— personal care, entertainment, restaurants, and the like. Remember, we're working to improve the quality of your life, not diminish it. In fact, this point is so important that not only do I suggest that you resist any downward adjustment in these categories, but that you consider increasing them. Examine the duller and more mundane ones or those you view as necessary but unappealing overhead. See if you can trim them at all. If you can, then distribute the difference among the categories that give you pleasure.

There's one exception to this principle of shifting money to areas of personal pleasure: If grandiosity, entitlement, or using money as a mood-changer are part of your history and have led to extravagant spending on yourself, then you'll want to make a reverse redistribution and start to rein in that destructive spending. Don't worry. You won't be deprived. Eventually you'll increase your spending across the entire spectrum of categories, just like everyone else. But then you'll do it on a realistic basis, as an authentic source of pleasure, rather than to gain the illusion of pleasure or for a temporary rush that only gets you deeper into debt.

Ex Post Facto

At the end of this coming month, use the last three columns in your combination plan and record as an index to measure how well you did and to help formulate your new plan for the next month.

Here, for the sake of simplicity, you can round off the amounts in the last three columns to the nearest dollar, as in the example that follows. Rounding off on your daily and weekly entries could lead to a significant discrepancy because of the large number of entries involved, but here it won't make more than a dollar or two's difference each month.

Add up the four weekly totals in each category to arrive at a monthly total. Enter those figures in the "Actual" column. Now compare the "Actual" entry in each category with the "Plan" entry for that category. Enter the difference in the

"+ or −" column. This represents how much more you spent than you had planned to (+, or plus), or how much less (−, or minus).

For example:

WEEK	1	2	3	4	ACTUAL	PLAN	+ OR −
Clothes	40.33	26.82	137.97	18.00	223	120	+103

In this example, you had planned to spend $120 on clothes last month. But you actually spent $223. So you entered +103 in the "+ or −" column, indicating that you went over your plan for this category by $103. That entry will now help you decide how much you want to spend in this category this month. You may, for example, want to compensate for overspending on clothes last month by spending nothing at all in that category this month, or keeping the amount to $20 or $25. Follow this same procedure with each of your categories, making whatever adjustments you think appropriate.

Don't put off making a Spending Plan. Do it as soon as you have completed one full month of the Spending Record, which you will use as a guide. And while you plan your expenses, remember that their total for the month should not exceed the total of your income, even by $15. If you plan to spend $15 more than you make, and you *do* spend that, there is only one possible result—debt. And one day at a time, you don't debt anymore.

11

COUPLES AND FAMILIES

When you're freeing yourself from debt in the context of a couple or a family, you face dynamics not encountered by people who live alone. This chapter provides techniques that specifically address those dynamics. If you're not part of a couple or family and would like to move directly to Chapter 12, go ahead, though I suggest you read this chapter anyway. You might well find material here that you can put to good use in your own life.

There are three basic configurations possible for those who live with others: couple, family, and single-parent family. The most important point to make about all of them is that within them the basic mechanisms of liberation remain the same as for people who live alone. You can't free yourself from debt by incurring new debt to get dental braces for your daughter any more than someone who is single can by incurring it to fly off to the islands on holiday.

Certainly the process can be more challenging when you're part of a couple or a family, and painful in ways not experienced by those who live alone. But not *extraordinarily* more challenging, nor *extraordinarily* more painful. Further, differences in temperament, experience, and other areas will make the distinction largely meaningless in many cases. Freeing yourself from debt will be harder for you than for some, easier than for others. That's the way it will always be—for you, me, and everyone else. Qualitatively, our experiences will be about the same.

But what about differences between the sexes—don't they affect the process? What differences do exist—biological, cultural, historical, perhaps even emotional and psychological—will affect the manner and style in which you free yourself, but less so than your personality and character will. The concepts and techniques of liberation are for *human beings*, not sexes. Debting is no more gender specific than alcoholism is; nor is liberation from it.

This chapter is divided into four sections: Couples, Families, Single-Parent Families, and In Closing. For people with children, each is relevant.

Couples

J'Accuse

"It's his fault."

"Her fault."

"If she'd only go to work, everything would be all right."

"If he didn't spend so much, we wouldn't have these problems."

Debtors are often very sensitive to their partner's debting, especially when that partner is also a debtor (not uncommon). They're certain their partner's debting is the chief cause of the financial trouble in the relationship, that they themselves are unfairly burdened, and that if their partner would only straighten up and stop debting, or pull his or her own weight—or even just a bit more than now—they would be all right as a couple and wouldn't have these problems.

It may be true that your partner *does* have a problem with debting and that it *is* contributing to the difficulties in the relationship, may even be the primary cause. But that doesn't mean it is the only cause or that without it your troubles with debt as a couple would end or at least become manageable. If you are a debtor yourself, the trouble would continue, and it would then be *your* debting that would become the major contributor to it.

Sometimes a debtor uses his partner's debting as camouflage for his own or to fuel his denial that *he* has a problem with debting. This is especially true when his partner's debting is more vivid or severe than his own. It's possible that you think you've been reading this book for your partner's benefit, nodding your head as you recognize her on this page or that or hoping he'll be able to see the problem for himself once you tell him about it or give him the book.

Uh-huh.

The fact is, you're not likely to have picked up this book or to have read this far in it if you weren't a debtor yourself. It's *possible*, but not likely. Here is a truth:

You can never force, or cause, anyone else to recover from debting.

You can only get free of it yourself. What *can* happen is that when you undertake to liberate yourself, then your partner, after some time in which to observe the changes in your life, eventually will too. (We'll discuss your options when this is not the case in the last section of this chapter.)

In another scenario, your partner may not be a debtor at all, may handle money very sensibly, in fact, or at least without causing harm. In this case, you are probably reluctant to admit to your own debting and instead present a host of "reasons" to explain or justify why you *had* to incur this debt. You may be depressed or angry over this or resentful of your partner, and accuse her of not being sensitive to or understanding you.

In yet another case, you might consciously or unconsciously, alone or in concert with your partner, arrange for him to do the debting in your household. That way, you or both of you together can maintain the illusion that *you* don't have a problem, that he does.

Whatever the circumstance, debt is a troublesome issue in your household, you're convinced that your partner bears the major responsibility for the problem, and you are quick to accuse him or her of that.

Conclave

The best way for you and your partner to begin to form a new relationship together with money is through Conclave. Conclave is a structured process that enables you to tell each other what you think or feel about yourselves and money, and about both of you together with money, without risk of fear, blame, or anger. It's also a potent technique to use later on to defuse potentially explosive confrontations over money.

To conduct a Conclave: Decide who will go first (A) and who second (B). Agree that whoever is speaking will stick to the format, and that the partner will listen attentively and respond only with: "Thank you."

Sit in chairs facing each other, close enough so that your knees are almost touching. Look directly into your partner's eyes while he is speaking.

The process has five parts.

In the first, A tells B the *three things* he likes *most* about *himself* with money. As A makes each statement, his partner—listening closely—acknowledges that she has heard him, understood him, and appreciates his having shared this with her by saying, "Thank you."

Only "Thank you"—nothing more, nothing less.

The process looks like this:

A: One of the things I like most about myself with money is that I'm generous with it.

B: Thank you.

A: Another thing I like most about myself with money is that I'm not afraid of it.

B: Thank you.

A: Another thing I like most about myself with money is that I save some.

B: Thank you.

Now, in the second part, A continues by telling B the *two things* he likes *least* about *himself* with money. Again, B answers only with "Thank you." For example:

A: One of the things I like least about myself with money is that I think I'm obsessive about it.

B: Thank you.

A: The other thing I like least about myself with money is that sometimes I still think I don't deserve any.

B: Thank you.

Next, A tells B the *three things* he likes *best* about *them* with money. Not about her, but about them, together. For example:

A: One of the things I like best about us with money is that we buy each other little presents.

B: Thank you.

A: Another thing I like best about us with money is that we balance our checkbooks, at least most of the time.

B: Thank you.

A: The other thing I like best about us with money is that we're beginning to look at it with the idea of making positive change.

B: Thank you.

Next, A tells B the *two things* he likes *least* about *them* with money. Again, not about her—but about them, together. It might look like this:

A: One thing I like least about us with money is that we sometimes get defensive or upset when we talk about it.

B: Thank you.

A: The other thing I like least about us with money is that we don't talk about it enough.

B: Thank you.

Finally, A tells B the *one thing* he would *most like to see come about* with *them* about money. Note that he isn't saying this is something he'd like to change about them but rather something he'd like to see come about—to happen, to evolve. Note also that he isn't saying this is something he'd like to see come about with her, but that he would like to see come about with them. For example:

A: The one thing I'd most like to see come about with us about money is that we grow more comfortable with each other in talking about it.

B: Thank you.

That's the end of A's part.

When A concludes, both of you should take a breath, lean back, and relax. Perhaps you'd like to stretch, take another breath. When you're ready, begin again, this time reversing your roles: Now B goes through the process, telling A what she likes most and then least about herself with money, about them together with money, and what she would most like to see come about with them and money. After each of her statements, her partner responds only with "Thank you."

It's important to follow the model above. The structure and phrasing are carefully designed to prevent blame or criticism from creeping in. They also emphasize what is liked most rather than least, which helps keep the focus on the positive. It's important, too, for the partner who is listening to respond with *nothing more* than "Thank you." No comments, no argument. No agreement or disagreement. No helpful suggestions, no interested discussion. Only: "Thank you." This provides acknowledgment of the communication and appreciation of its intimacy but prevents any possibility of judgment.

To further protect the process, agree beforehand that neither of you will try to discuss anything that might come up in it for at least twenty-four hours. You might want to end by giving each other a hug, and perhaps holding each other for a moment.

Conclave prepares the way for you and your partner to take the next step, which is detailed in the following two topics. Later it can help you maintain a healthy awareness of yourself and your partner in relationship to money and of your strengths and weaknesses as a couple in handling it. Hold your first Conclave early, then whenever else you think it might be helpful.

Now We Two Are Three
(At Least in This Respect)

"And now we two are one" . . . goes an old wedding song.

Nice, romantic. Very loving. Spiritual. Only it doesn't work—not when money is involved and one or both partners are debtors. In fact, trying to pool your money into a communal pot in such a situation can be catastrophic, breeding anger, fear, jealousy, blame, resentment—and those just for openers.

The song to sing, paraphrasing Fats Domino, is: "Just honey and me, and the household makes three."

Because there are *my* expenses, *your* expenses, and the *house's* expenses. The house's (or household expenses) are those we have in common, which are necessary to us as a couple and that benefit us both: rent or mortgage payment, the money we spend on food, on electricity, car payments, and the like. What is needed in any couple are three Spending Plans—one for you, one for me, and one for the house. So the next step is to address that.

The Household Spending Plan

Yours, Mine, and the House's You've made a Spending Plan for yourself. You're enthused, you love the idea of getting free of debt. You feel better about yourself and about us than you have for a long time. You're hopeful. Now, how do you get me to make a Spending Plan for myself?

The bad news is, you don't. You can't get me to, or make me, do anything. What you *can* do is share your enthusiasm with me and explain in a caring, nonbelligerent way why you think it would be helpful to you, to me, and to us as a couple, for me to draw up such a plan, and then hope for the best. If I resist this or any other part of Back to the Black, and you harp at or badger me, the situation will deteriorate and our relationship probably will just get worse. Sad, but true.

But let's say for now that I do see the sense of this and do make a Spending Plan of my own. We may wish to share our plans with each other, we may not. Your plan is yours, and what you choose to do with your money is really none of my business. My plan is mine, and what I choose to do with my money is really none of your business. That may be hard for either of you or both of you to accept at first, but it's important that you do. Each of us is entitled to privacy here if we wish it, and at least a certain amount of privacy is generally healthy.

But the house's Spending Plan is a different story. That is very much *both* of our business, and it needs to be if we're to have any hope of positive change at all.

Drawing Up the House's Plan Even if I refuse to draw up a Spending Plan of my own, I might still see the sense in us sitting down together to draw up one for the house, covering *our* expenses. If I don't, perhaps you can persuade me to do it anyway, as a bit of practical help I can give you in what you're doing.

(Perhaps you *can't* persuade me. Maybe I'm deeply opposed to all this—for whatever reasons—and refuse even to discuss the subject with you. What then? There are options, some happier than others, that we'll discuss later. For now, let's assume that I am willing.)

Couples differ in what they designate shared expenses as opposed to personal expenses and in how they apportion those between themselves. The first task is to list all of the *household's* expenses. The electric bill, for example, is a household expense. Your perfume is your expense; my running shoes, my expense; and each of us is responsible for our own haircuts. Here are some expenses that most couples consider to be household expenses:

- Cabs (if taken together)
- Car
- Children's expenses
- Gas/electricity
- Groceries
- Home equipment
- Home furnishings
- Home heating
- Home repair/maintenance
- Home supplies
- Housecleaning
- Investments
- Life insurance (if married)
- Medical insurance (if married)
- Property taxes
- Pet
- Rent/mortgage
- Telephone
- Vacation/travel
- Miscellaneous

Use or modify any of these for your own Household Spending Plan and add any not mentioned that you need.

Apportioning Expenses How do you apportion household expenses honestly and fairly between you? Ideally you and your partner would each pay fifty percent of these shared expenses, and in many cases (especially in couples without children), that is what actually happens or eventually happens. But in others it is neither reasonable nor possible. We can't make definitive statements about this, but we can provide general guidelines. If you follow the five principles below, you'll be able to divide up your common expenses successfully.

First: Do the apportioning within the framework of this entire program, with a knowledge and understanding of all its concepts and techniques. Do it out of commitment to your recovery and with respect and regard for your partner. To help in that, don't try to draw up a Household Spending Plan until you've read through to the end of the book.

Second: Each partner's contribution should be at least equivalent to what he or she would have to spend in order to be self-supporting if living alone. Not necessarily in the style in which you both are now, but at least in one that would be reasonable and humane.

Third: Acknowledge any legitimate discrepancy that exists between your incomes. A legitimate discrepancy is one that results from the realities of life rather than from one partner's simply not wanting to work or from compulsive spending. For example: You are both debtors, both recovering from that. You are a medical doctor. Your husband is a professor of English literature. You're earning four times the income he is—and can. Here, it is reasonable for you to pay a greater share of the household expenses than he does; perhaps even as high as eighty percent, especially for lifestyle choices such as vacations or dining out. (In some categories, it may be reasonable for you to pay one hundred percent.) Of course, the reverse is true too. If your partner earns four times what you do, and for legitimate reasons, then it's reasonable for him to be paying a larger percentage of the shared expenses.

Fourth: Factor into your Household Spending Plan the work either of you does around the house that's necessary to daily living. This might include cooking, cleaning, child-watching, lawn-mowing, house maintenance, and the like. Factor it in as a cash contribution. (How to do that will be explained later in the chapter.)

Fifth: If you need to, use a progressive scale of apportionment—one linked to time. In this method the partner who has been under-contributing pays a bit more each month until he or she reaches a certain level. Frank and Ellen are both debtors, and getting free of that together. Since in the past Frank had been fully employed while Ellen had worked only occasional part-time jobs, wanting to pursue a career as an actress, Frank had done most of the debting for them, using his credit cards to finance their vacations, opening the store accounts in his name, borrowing the money for them when they were short, and making the payment arrangements with service providers. He had also been paying $1,000 of their rent, which was $1,200 a month. When Frank and Ellen drew up their Household Spending Plan, they agreed that Ellen would raise her contribution to the rent by $50 a month until she was paying a full half of it, which took eight months to achieve.

This method can be especially useful when one partner's contributions have been practically nonexistent. It also works well with a debtor who lives alone and has been subsidized by parents up to now. You can apply it to all shared expenses or only to some. The simplest way to make a Household Spending Plan is to keep a Household Spending Record for a month, logging all the expenses the house incurs, then use that as a guide in creating a plan.

Matching Your Personal Plan to Your Household Plan Reconciling your personal Spending Plan to your Household Spending Plan is fairly simple. Your personal plan should include, in addition to your strictly personal categories, all the household categories to which you contribute too. For example, if you contribute $600 to the household as your share of its $1,200 rent, then you *personally* are spending $600 a month on rent—and that should be noted in your personal plan. If the household spends $500 a month on groceries and your share of the house expenses is fifty percent, then you *personally* are spending $250 a month on groceries—and that should be noted in your personal plan. So also with every other household category.

It might seem simpler at first just to lump all those different expenses into one category called "Household" on your personal plan and enter the total there. But that would deprive you of clarity. You wouldn't really know where the money is going, only *that* it is going.

Here are some categories most couples consider to be personal expenses:

- Alimony
- Books
- Cabs (if taken alone)
- Car (if it's your own)
- Charitable contributions
- Child support
- Clothes
- Cosmetics
- Dry cleaning
- Education
- Food out (if eaten alone: fast food, diners)
- Gifts (to each other, or to personal friends)
- Haircuts/beauty salon
- Hobby

- Income taxes (if assessed beyond amount withheld; adjusted for joint-filing rates if married)
- Life insurance (if not married)
- Magazines/newspapers
- Medical (doctors, prescriptions, glasses)
- Medical insurance (if not married)
- Personal care
- Personal growth
- Professional dues
- Sports
- Therapy
- Tuition
- Union dues
- Vacation/travel (if taken alone)
- Vitamins

A particular couple may consider any of these to be a shared expense. Agreement is what matters most here.

The Rule of Three

The Rule of Three says that both partners will probably be happier, that there will be more peace in the relationship, and that liberation will be facilitated when there are three separate checking accounts and three separate savings accounts—when each partner has his own and her own personal checking account and savings account, and when the house has its own two accounts. These latter, the household accounts, are held jointly by both partners, and all the shared expenses are paid directly out of them. This arrangement makes perfectly clear what is the household's money and what is not. It provides both partners a sense of privacy and independence, and it helps a debtor gain a more accurate vision of his or her real circumstances.

Summit Meeting

After you've established a Household Spending Plan, schedule a series of Summit Meetings together. A Summit Meeting is a semiformal conference in which the two of you sit down together to discuss everything that's pertinent to the household's finances and make any decisions required. After you've taken care of the household's needs, each of you should be free to discuss anything with your partner about your own finances that you'd like to or about which you would like some feedback.

It's best to hold a Summit Meeting once a week for the first few months. Saturday or Sunday after breakfast is often a good time. Later you can meet on whatever schedule keeps things running smoothly. Many couples make twice-monthly meetings a regular part of their life. They're an effective way to communicate on an ongoing basis about shared expenses and any questions or problems that might arise.

The Wet Tub Discussion

Sooner or later something will come up between you and your partner about money that is particularly difficult—too charged to try to resolve in a regular Summit Meeting or deal with through a Conclave. The Wet Tub Discussion is a good way to defuse the situation. It allows you to talk the problem over with minimal rancor and helps you to find a happy and workable solution. Here's how to do it:

1. Fill a bathtub two-thirds with warm water.
2. Take off your clothes, each of you.
3. Get into the tub together facing each other.
4. Smile at each other for ten seconds.
5. Begin your discussion.

It's very difficult to become angry with someone when you're sitting naked in a tub of warm water with him or her.

Many people laugh self-consciously at this suggestion at first, but nearly everyone who tries it finds it helps them to say what they want to in a way that is neither threatening nor accusatory, that it encourages openness, and that it makes it easier for both partners to treat each other with care and affection.

Limit your tub time to about half an hour. If you can't resolve the situation in that time, set it aside till the next day, then repeat the procedure. Most situations can be cleared up in one or two sessions. Occasionally you might want to practice this technique even when you don't have anything difficult to discuss, just for the hell of it.

Families

What differentiates a couple from a family?

Children.

Children make it necessary for a couple—now a family—to address concerns that childless couples don't need to, just as those couples have to deal with issues not faced by debtors who live alone. (The fact remains, though, that families and couples can't free themselves from debting; only *individuals* can. While anyone's recovery will benefit the people around her, that recovery must be singular.)

Children have needs. Some of those needs are financial. Since children cannot meet those needs by themselves, then you must. Therefore, your children's financial needs are *your* financial needs—just like any others you have. And their expenses are *your* expenses—just like any others you have. There's no way around this. If you are tempted to feel uncommonly burdened by it, remember: Your situation is no different from that of any other debtor, more difficult than some, less difficult than others.

Back to the Black has no philosophic or political opinion about how a family ought to organize itself or manage its finances. The concepts and techniques that follow are offered only as ways to help you become free of debting.

Accord

To reach accord is to come into agreement or harmony. It's what nations do—ideally. Sometimes they do it at summit meetings. You and your partner need to reach accord, too, over every question that either of you has concerning your children's expenses. The only *general* point to make about such expenses is that they belong in the Household Spending Plan (except sometimes in the case of children from a previous marriage, as we'll discuss). A simple way to deal with them clearly is to create a category called "Children" in your Household Spending Plan, then break that down into subcategories such as "Clothes," "Medical," "Toys," and the like.

Matters over which you and your partner need to reach accord might include situations like this: You have to pay a big chunk of your monthly income in alimony and child support—should this be reflected in the amount you are expected to contribute to household expenses? Or the reverse: You *receive* alimony and child support every month—should *this* be reflected in the amount you are expected to contribute to household expenses?

George and Sarah live together. Both work in television and both make about the same amount of money. George has two children from an earlier marriage. He pays child support for his youngest and most of the college tuition for his eldest. The accord he and Sarah reached was that she would contribute sixty percent to their shared household expenses and he forty percent.

Richard, a data processor, is married to Gina, an organist and choirmaster. Richard, like George, pays child support for a son from an earlier marriage. He also makes more money than Gina does or can in her field. Gina has a daughter from a previous marriage of her own, who lives with them. Their accord called for them to include Gina's daughter in their household plan, for Gina to place into the household fund the money she received in child support from her former husband, and for each of them then to contribute fifty percent of the remaining household needs.

Questions can arise over apportioning food and entertainment expenses when children from a former marriage come to visit for the weekend. There will also be issues that don't involve children but are similar in that they have no clear and immediately apparent answer that require accord too.

Ben and Jeanine, for example, put their telephone expenses in their Household Spending Plan, as most couples do. But Jeanine liked to make long calls to old college friends in other cities, which resulted in high phone bills. Ben, who was contributing fifty-five percent of the household's expenses, felt abused and taken advantage of in this. He wanted Jeanine to stop making the calls. Jeanine felt controlled and bullied. This was a source of friction between them for weeks, until they agreed to sit down together at a Summit Meeting and not to get up until they had reached accord. The accord they reached was to keep a log book next to the telephone and enter into it every long-distance number they dialed. When the bill arrived each month, they matched the numbers on it against the log book, and each paid for his or her own long-distance calls. They were both satisfied with this.

There aren't any hard-and-fast rules about accord—only a need to reach it over any financial issue that is divisive or causing either of you to feel resentful or victimized. In sitting down to reach accord, do so as best you can with the spirit of the whole of Back to the Black in mind.

What's It Worth?

In most families, one partner puts in more time working on the household's behalf than the other, sometimes much more time. Traditionally, this has been the female partner. That's not always the case now, but it's still more true than not and probably will be for a while. For our purposes, though, who does this is irrelevant. What is relevant is how that fact is acknowledged.

Hours spent working on behalf of the household—or rather the *cash value* of those hours—need to be recognized as a contribution to the Household Spending Plan, and one that's every bit as real as if the partner who worked them had written a check to the household. The best way to handle this is for you and your partner to arrive at a figure that is agreeable to both of you through casual discussion. If you think it would be helpful to approach the question more formally, here are four simple guidelines you might use.

First: Begin by recognizing that your time—as the time of a human being—is neither more valuable nor less valuable than your partner's time. Your *earning power* per hour or day may be different, but the *absolute value* of that hour or day, as a unit of time, is not. Your time, as the time of a human being, is worth exactly the same as your partner's. One hour equals one hour, regardless of who works it or how much he or she can command for it on the market.

Second: Estimate the number of work-hours your household requires in order to keep functioning well. Restrict these to *true* work-hours, such as shopping, lawn-mowing, or caring for young children. Don't include time spent doing the things we all do for ourselves or for each other as a matter of course, such as picking up after ourselves or playing with our children. A simplified reckoning might look something like:

HOUSEHOLD REQUIREMENTS
WEEKLY

10 child-care hours
8 shopping hours
12 cooking hours
5 house maintenance/repair hours
11 housecleaning hours

46 TOTAL

In most cases, these work-hours should be considered your joint responsibility, in equal parts, regardless of how you apportion your household *cash* expenses. But that doesn't mean you have to work these hours in equal parts if you don't want to. The third guideline offers a fair way to modify a fifty-fifty contribution.

Third: If you wish not to work household hours in equal parts, the first step is to calculate the financial value of those hours. That's easy to do. Examine the want ads in your local newspaper to see what kind of wages are being offered for these services, or survey friends who hire people to do such things for them. Child care, for example, might be worth from $5 to $20 an hour depending on where you live and the care desired. Let's say that the going rate in your area is $9. Let's say you could hire someone to do your grocery shopping for you for $7 an hour. Cooking, $20. Work around the house such as painting or window-puttying, $20. Housecleaning, $12. So now we have something that looks like:

HOUSEHOLD REQUIREMENTS
WEEKLY

10 child-care hours	@	$9	=	$90
8 shopping hours	@	7	=	56
12 cooking hours	@	20	=	240

5 house maintenance/				
repair hours	@	20	=	100
11 cleaning hours	@	12	=	132
				$618

Peter and Kelly have two children. Let's say, in the schedule above, that Kelly is putting in all the household hours except those spent on repair and maintenance, which Peter does. That means that Kelly—who is doing thirty-four hours of various kinds of work for the household each week, worth from $7 to $20 an hour on the market—is contributing $518 of the total $618 worth of services their household requires. Peter, who is putting in five hours a week of house repair and maintenance, which is worth $20 an hour on the market, is contributing $100 worth.

Since Peter and Kelly are each individually responsible for contributing 23 hours—or $309 worth—of services to the house, then Kelly is not only meeting her share but is contributing another $209 worth on top of it.

$518 (Kelly's actual contribution)
−309 (Kelly's responsibility)
$209 (extra amount Kelly has contributed)

To correct this imbalance, Kelly should be given credit for having already contributed $209 in cash to the household for the week, and Peter should put in an extra $209 (since Kelly has done $209 worth of what can be considered *his* household work).

If we continue this example through the month, it would mean, since there are 4.3 weeks in a month, that Peter would contribute $899 more in cash beyond what he normally would, and Kelly $899 less ($209 per week × 4.3 weeks = $899).

If their household's monthly cash expenses are $2,500,

and Peter and Kelly have apportioned those expenses equally, then each would be responsible for contributing $1,250. Each would *also* be responsible for performing 98.9 hours of household tasks per month. But Kelly has already performed not only her own share of household work, but $899 worth of Peter's too. Peter, therefore, will contribute $2,149 in actual cash toward the month's expenses, and Kelly $351.

If the math here confuses you, don't worry about it. You don't need to master this formula or any other in order to work out a fair arrangement over household work-hours. All that's necessary is for you to be easy and clear with each other and to approach the process in good faith, with mutual respect and affection. Given that, you'll be able to come up with a good plan together.

Fourth: Should one of you utterly refuse to perform any of the necessary household tasks at all, for any reason—from domestic politics to arcane religious beliefs—there is still a simple solution. He or she can contribute an appropriately larger share of cash to the household, as in the example above, or hire someone else to perform them. In the latter case, of course, that partner would pay for such help out of his or her personal Spending Plan.

"Well, damn it, if she's not going to do any of the household work herself, then I'm not going to either!"

Okay, then you can *both* hire others to do it.

Many variations are possible here. The household might hire people to do the housecleaning and lawn-mowing, while the partners perform the rest of the tasks themselves—or practically any other combination you can think of.

Swiss Family Robinson-ing It

The Swiss Family Robinson, by nineteenth-century Swiss writer J. D. Wyss, is an adventure novel about a shipwrecked family, children and parents, that has to pull together on the island where they find themselves washed up, first to survive, then finally to triumph. The story has been a favorite in Western literature for almost two centuries. Today most people know it through the popular Walt Disney movie of 1960.

In the Swiss Family Robinson technique, you enlist your entire family into the cause of freeing yourself from debt and make the process, as best you can, into an adventure.

(I know: Debting is *always* singular. But in some cases, to a limited extent, the family can be looked upon as a debting unit, especially when both parents are debtors, or in single-parent families, which means that in some ways it can work as a unit toward liberation.)

Be honest with your children. Explain to them, according to their level of comprehension, what the situation is and what you're setting out to accomplish. Phrase this positively. Be careful not to say anything that will alarm or frighten them, especially if they're young. (And indeed there *is* nothing alarming or frightening—you're getting free of debt now, not falling deeper into it.) It's not necessary to go into detail. Just give them the essence: Here's where we are, here's what we want to do, and here are some of the ways we're going to do it.

If you'd like, include the children in your Summit Meetings, or in some of them. Whatever you do, be sure to give them a sense of real participation—helping to plan, being able to volunteer ideas, having a vote, monitoring progress with you, participating in resolving questions that come up.

David and Carole's children were twelve, nine, and seven when the family undertook this technique. Together, infused with all the feeling of adventure that David and Carole could bring to it, the family divided up the household tasks, created a system to recognize and celebrate one another's accomplishments, met at a family Summit Meeting twice each month (with David and Carole meeting alone on alternate weeks), and made as many decisions as possible by vote.

"Carole and I felt we didn't have to lie or hide anything from the children," David says. "They understood and accepted things I never would have expected them to. Since they had a say and knew some of the *whys* and saw us all as a team, they didn't object much to missing out on some of the stuff their friends had or did or pitching in to help. Sometimes they were outright enthusiastic."

If your children are older, in their late teens, candor is probably the only element of this technique that is helpful. How much detail you wish to go into with them will depend on you, them, and your relationship with them. At the very least, have some kind of open discussion of family finances with them—what's possible, what isn't, and why.

In the early days of my own recovery from debt, my discretionary money was very limited. At that time, I had my youngest son with me every other weekend. I talked with him honestly about my finances, and the fact that I was getting myself out of debt, and shared with him some of steps I was taking to accomplish that. He understood. He joined with me in shopping and cooking, hunting through the newspapers for places to go and activities to do that we would both enjoy and that weren't costly. We had very good times together and were close.

Could we have had equally good times, and been equally close, if I'd been able to take us to Belize for a week of scuba diving, or out to dinner frequently, or to the theater? I like to think so. But I *know* we had good times then, and that we *were* close. And I cherish those times in memory, particularly now that he is grown up and living three thousand miles away in California. I wouldn't at all mind living one of those weekends again when we went to the farmer's market at Union Square on Saturday morning, and cooked a pot of curried rice with onions and raisins, and played board games, and took the subway up to the Broadcasting Museum on East Fifty-third Street to watch old television shows from the 1950s. I wouldn't mind it at all.

My God, Me as Enabler?

Be careful not to become, or continue to be, an enabler in your family. You can enable your partner to keep debting by giving him money, by paying her bills, or by putting more than your share of money into the household accounts to make up for him putting in less than his. If you're the parent of an adult child who is also a debtor, either living with you or not, you can fall into enabling her the same way.

Back to the Black is not about your partner getting free of debt, or your child, or anyone else. It's about *you* getting free. If you begin or continue to enable someone else, not only are you actually harming rather than helping him, but sooner or later your enabling will put a strain on your own recovery.

It may be hard for you to see at this point how you as a debtor yourself could enable someone else. But people do find ways, especially when they're getting better. Most often they're motivated by compassion. They make excuses for their mate or grown child and bail him out—and again, and then again. But this isn't help, it's enabling, and well-intentioned or not, it's toxic to both parties. The kindest thing you can do for a debtor is to stop shielding her from the consequences of her debting.

Single-Parent Families

If you haven't read the sections on COUPLES and FAMILIES earlier in this chapter, please go back and read them now. Most of the material there applies to you, even if you're the head of a single-parent family.

This section does not offer a special plan for the head of a single-parent family to get out of debt, no more than the preceding sections offered specialized plans for people who are part of a couple or a family. Rather, it provides specific techniques that a debtor who's also the head of a single-parent family can use in addition to those in the rest of Back to the Black. The operative description here is *debtor*, not single parent.

Most single-parent families are still headed by women, though the number of men who head such families is increasing. These techniques, like all the others in the book, remain the same regardless of your sex.

Co-oping

Create a network with other heads of single-parent families. While barter is generally counterproductive for debtors in the long run—it subtly reinforces the idea that you can't earn enough to take care of your needs—here it can be very helpful, and especially in the beginning. Trade what you have that others in the network might want for whatever they might have that you need.

Clothes, furniture, and similar items that are in good condition can be passed from a household whose children have outgrown them to another whose children are just growing into them. Prices on everything from clothes to appliances and automobiles can sometimes be reduced by offering to make bulk or multiple purchases.

Three single mothers in Delray Beach, Florida, for example, who needed to replace their family automobiles, went separately to the used-car division of a dealer upon whom they had agreed. Each picked the car she wanted, negotiated the best price she could, but then declined to buy it and said she wanted to think about it. Then they returned to the dealer together—and in exchange for offering to buy all three cars were able to get an additional six percent discount on each car.

Child-watching hours can often be arranged as a swap, to be repaid in kind. Out of the camaraderie that can grow in a single-parent network, people sometimes exchange professional work or services too—carpentry, dentistry, bookkeeping, nearly anything that one member specializes in and another needs.

Teaming up to rent an apartment or house and forming a kind of extended family is another form of co-oping. Jane, who had a three-year-old son, moved with Sasha, who had two daughters, fourteen and eleven, into a small house. They lived there for nearly two years, at a household cost significantly lower than what either would have had to pay alone, and each had someone with whom to share the adult tasks.

Where can you find other single parents with whom to form a network? Through your church or synagogue. Through community associations and organizations. Through men's groups or women's groups. By meeting them at playgrounds or children's events. Through community newspapers, newsletters, and building bulletin boards. In a self-help program. Through school guidance counselors, your pediatrician, and friends.

You're Entitled

You Are Entitled to Use Every Resource Available to You and to Receive Every Benefit for Which You're Qualified.

Just because you have stopped debting—which is a spectacular achievement—and are committed to continuing that way, doesn't mean that you have to turn down help.

No one likes to feel weak or dependent. And debtors who are now getting free of debt and debting sometimes become sensitive to and unhappy and uncomfortable with having others provide them with what they need. Living solvently now—not debting one day a time—they find it difficult to ask for help or to accept it, thinking they ought to be able to do everything for themselves immediately, or because they fear it would mean slipping back, or because they *want* the help, which makes them feel guilty.

Here is something you need always to keep in mind: If

what you do does not involve incurring new debt, then whatever else it may be, it's not debting. What's more, if it is something that will help make the process of freeing yourself from debt and debting easier, then it is desirable to do. Since it is in the service of your liberation, it should be a source of self-esteem rather than embarrassment or shame; it took courage and commitment to do it.

The range of resources available to you can be great, depending upon your situation. Some people are qualified for government assistance such as unemployment benefits, Medicaid, food stamps, housing supplements, aid to dependent children, Social Security payments, and the like. Many corporations have employee assistance programs. There are private agencies, such as Volunteer Lawyers for the Arts. Unions sometimes help with goods, money, and scholarships. Community centers may provide counseling services or a place where children can stay after school. The Legal Aid Society often represents tenants under threat of eviction.

Sharon, a graphic designer with two children, exhausted what little savings she had during her bitterly contested divorce. Her estranged husband, who was punitive and obsessive, sued for custody of their children. Sharon went more than $30,000 into debt to her lawyer before, as the first major step in freeing herself from debting, she resolved not to incur any new debt—no matter what she had to do. Briefly, she represented herself in court. But she was frightened by that and didn't do well. Through a friend, she made contact with a shelter for battered women. Though emotionally abused during her marriage, Sharon had never been physically abused. Ordinarily the shelter did not help in such cases, but because of Sharon's persistent entreaties, it finally did refer her to a lawyer. He examined her situation and agreed to represent her pro bono. Thus Sharon was able to get what she needed for herself and her children without incurring any new debt, which was a crucial step in her recovery. Since then, she has been able to raise her income steadily and has even begun, on a small level, to repay her previous debts.

Seeking to learn what help is available, then asking for it (and in some cases becoming willing to accept it) is not easy. But it *is* self-care, it *is* a step forward, and you *are* entitled to it. By availing yourself of it, you assist and strengthen your recovery. You'll give back much more than you receive. You'll give it back through your recovery. You'll give it back to everyone with whom you come into contact. Your recovery will become a part of what is positive in the world.

What's Right Is Right

Sue the (expletive deleted).

If he ran out on you and stuck you with bills, if she looted your joint bank account, if he or she charged your credit card and store accounts up to the maximum and left you to pay for everything, or dumped the children on you or won't help with their support, then it's time to get tough.

I am in favor of, and to the best of my ability practice, looking upon all beings with eyes of compassion. Nevertheless, and not contradictorily, I am also in favor of requesting, and forcing if necessary and when possible, all beings to honor their financial responsibilities to their former spouses and the children they sired or bore.

This kind of assistance is *owed* to you by your former partner. You are entitled to it, and in an amount that fairly represents your situation and his or hers.

Maybe your partner has skipped out and you don't know where he is. That happens. But finding someone is usually easier than most people think. The simplest, most effective way to do it is to hire a private investigative agency, preferably one run by ex–law enforcement agents. You can find a reliable one through a friend or an attorney.

When you know where your former spouse is but he refuses to take responsibility, the courts may help. They're becoming increasingly firm in requiring noncustodial parents to pay their fair share of the costs of raising their children. Recently the federal government has indicated that it too may become involved in forcing such parents to meet their responsibilities.

There are no guarantees here. You might not be able to find your former spouse. The court may be unwilling or unable to compel her to pay for expenses charged to your joint accounts or to make an equitable contribution toward supporting your children. (You also need to weigh your potential legal costs against the possible benefits; sometimes the equation just isn't in your favor.) But whatever the ultimate results, take what sensible actions you can. What's right is right, and you are not unfair in asking for that principle to be upheld.

In Closing

Hardball and Optimism

Getting solvent is not for people who need it. It's for people who want it.

If you're married to or live with someone who is also a debtor but who won't admit that, or who refuses to take any steps toward recovery or even to cooperate with you in your own, not even to the simple extent, say, of drawing up a Household Spending Plan with you, then you're in a difficult situation.

Your best tack is optimism. Just go about your own liberation and assume that in time there will be a resolution that serves your best interests, individually and together. Assume that your own life will grow ever calmer, deeper, and richer because of your work, and that sooner or later your partner won't be able to help but notice and eventually to want a similar experience for himself or herself. Don't argue, plead, or cajole. Don't try to proselytize. None of that will work. Simply live your own recovery—for your own sake—in the knowledge that it is the best and most loving thing you can do for your partner.

Sometimes this tack works. Sometimes it doesn't. But regardless of what happens with your partner, this is the best thing you can do for *yourself.*

For a while.

Eventually there will come a time when it is no longer reasonable to assume that continuing in this fashion will result in a positive resolution. That time could be a year. It could be two years, or three. Or it could be a few months. Only you can determine that. But when it does arrive—if it does—you have a hard decision to make. If your partner will have nothing to do with getting free of debting, you have three choices:

One: Stay with him, in the knowledge that he will probably never change. Stay with the understanding that you are *choosing* this situation, that you recognize, comprehend, and accept it for what it is, that you voluntarily elect to remain in it. In this case, you probably perceive more that is good in the circumstance than bad, deem it livable as it is, and believe you can undertake your own recovery in its context without impossible difficulty.

Two: Try to persuade your partner to change. You might negotiate, for example, trading an activity she would like you to do, or to cease doing, in exchange for her sitting down with you and drawing up a Household Spending Plan together. You could ask her to read this book, to go into counseling with you, or to a support group—even if only to listen and observe. Perhaps she would be willing to talk to a cleric or a friend about the problem. You might write her a long letter, expressing your love and explaining why you think such a change would be good for her and for you both as a couple.

This kind of approach is potentially explosive. So whatever you do, do it lovingly and as free of judgment and criticism as you can. Otherwise, your partner will probably only become angry and resist even more strenuously.

If you exhaust every option you can think of and there is no change, you can either accept the situation, as described earlier, decide to give it more time, or deliver an ultimatum, a warning that you find the situation intolerable and that unless your partner takes at least some steps toward trying to improve it, you are going to leave or do whatever is necessary to see that she leaves.

Three: Leave, or see that your partner does. This is an extremely serious step. I'm not suggesting that you take it. I present it here only as one of the three choices available to you. If you do consider leaving or causing your partner to leave, then do so carefully. Be aware of all the consequences and ramifications of such an act. Write them down so you can see them clearly. Talk to your cleric, therapist, or someone else you trust to be objective and to have your best interests at heart. Even in the few situations I've known where it was clearly in the best interest of the recovering debtor to end the relationship, it still, inescapably, involved a great deal of pain and upheaval.

Hardball is necessary, but optimism about it is always best. It will make things easier for you and for everyone else as well. Further, the very act of expecting a positive outcome will make such an outcome more likely.

Live and Let Live

Finally, live and let live. Live your own life, as you choose, and let your partner, your grown children, and everyone else you know live their lives as they choose—or for reasons beyond your ken, perhaps as they must. Attend to the beam in your own eye; the motes in theirs are their business. It is your birthright to live as you wish, it is theirs to do the same.

Your recovery depends only on you. Theirs, if they are debtors, depends only on them.

It is possible that we *do* know sometimes what is best for another adult. It is also possible that we don't. To assume that we do is arrogance, to try to force that assumption on someone is tyranny.

"Never try to teach a pig to think," goes an old maxim. "It won't work, and will only annoy the pig."

And every missionary looking at a pig is a pig looking at a missionary.

Therefore, be kind to yourself, and to everyone else: Live, and let live.

12

STABILIZING

If you follow the guidelines in the preceding chapters, you *can not* go any further into debt. If you don't go any further into debt, and if you follow the guidelines in this and the subsequent chapters, you will in time repay each and every one of your creditors and go on to live free of debt and with a sense of prosperity thereafter.

It's that simple.

The Spending Plan Redux

If you find that the total of your planned expenses exceeds that of your available money, something has to change. Otherwise you'll incur new debt, and that's not an option anymore. There are only two ways to correct such a disparity—cut your expenses or bring in more money. Generally, the solution is a combination of both.

There's often more fat in a given category than appears at first. Search out those that are clearly extravagant or disproportionate. If, for example, you plan to spend $400 on entertainment or restaurants, while your plan indicates that your expenses will exceed your income by $300, there is a clear need to trim $300 somewhere. You might prefer to leave your restaurant or entertainment category alone. You might want very much to spend $400 dining out or on the theater. Nothing says you can't—as long as you cut $300 from some other category or combination of them. It's your plan. You can put it together any way you like.

There *is* a way to pay for expenses that exceed income: You can draw upon assets—use money from a savings account, for example—to make up the difference. That's not debting. It's your money, you can do with it as you wish. However, it's not a particularly desirable tactic, since in effect you're losing ground instead of gaining it. But for now, if you truly need to use that money to avoid debting, by all means do so.

Here are some ways other people have cut expenses in various categories:

- Barter services such as baby-sitting.
- Carpool.
- Take buses instead of cabs.
- Walk instead of taking a bus.
- Go to the movies instead of the theater.
- Rent a videocassette instead of going to the movies.
- Entertain at home instead of taking people out.
- Travel by train instead of plane.
- Through a commercial delivery service, drive someone else's car to your destination, which covers travel expenses.
- Attend a state university instead of a private university.
- Wear last year's party dress a while longer.
- Use email or write letters instead of calling everyone long distance.
- Obtain a moratorium on debt repayments.
- Keep your daily spending record scrupulously.
- Cut down the frequency of nonessential services, such as lawn maintenance, or cancel them and do them yourself.

- Eat more meals at home instead of out.
- Give gifts of personal service or things you've created rather than buying them.
- Borrow books, records, and videocassettes from the library instead of buying or renting them.
- Apply for a reduction in alimony or child support.
- Stop smoking.
- Defer nonessential medical treatment.
- Use parks and public facilities for sports and exercise rather than private clubs.
- Use museums, galleries, aquariums, and free public events as part of your entertainment.
- Repair or have repaired damaged items such as clothes or appliances rather than buy new ones.
- Reupholster rather than replace furniture.
- Cut down the number of hours of household help.

Here are some of the ways other people have brought in more money:

- Sell something—anything at all.
- Take in a boarder or roommate.
- Put in overtime hours.
- Take a limited-hours second job.
- Do private tutoring.
- If you're not working at all, take a job.
- Liquidate an asset.
- Call in debts owed to you.
- Hold a garage sale.
- Do office temporary work.
- Sell any expertise you have on a consultancy basis or exercise a skill you possess for pay.
- Hold a rent party or similar event; one inventive woman with a flamboyant personality organized a "celebrity roast" of herself.

Again, like the others in this book, these lists are not and can not be all-inclusive. They're meant to stimulate your imagination. It's important for you to draw up your own lists, which reflect *your* needs and possibilities. Remember that the more you consciously break free of the restrictions in your old ways of thinking, the more valuable and effective your list-making will be. And keep in mind that early measures are just that—they're not life sentences.

Building a Margin

Stabilizing—making sure your expenses do not exceed your income—may be the zero point for you: Your expenses require every dollar you make. Fine. You're not going any further into debt. That in itself is remarkable progress. If you're on the plus side of zero, have a bit of surplus, terrific.

Do *not* pay a creditor with it.

Do *not* "treat" yourself with it.

Do *not* squirrel it away in a savings account.

Do spread a portion, maybe half, through those categories in your Spending Plan you'd most like to increase, paying particular attention to those that contribute to your pleasure and enjoyment of life.

Do put the remaining portion into some form of savings. That's the margin you want to begin building.

This margin will become your safety net, a contingency fund that will stand between you and unforeseen events that might make you think you're in jeopardy of debting. It will grow steadily.

Continue to follow this method of division each month in which you have a surplus. Don't be tempted to put it all into your contingency fund. Remember, this program isn't about bottom-line survival; it's about improving the quality of your life. You won't be allocating half your extra money to this fund forever. We'll discuss the nature and use of the contingency fund fully in Chapter 19, but for now just know that it doesn't take long to build one that is adequate.

No Margin?

No margin? Not yet, that's all. Or worse, still coming out short on monthly income? So far, that's all.

Study again the various measures through which other people have raised emergency money, cut expenses, and brought in additional income. If you haven't made your own lists yet, then do so now. They're quite valuable. To ignore them is to handicap yourself. Making them is a self-escalating process. The more you do it, the better and more imaginative you become, and the more effective and useful they become.

And one day at a time, just for today, do not debt.

Put what you've already learned into practice—the margin will appear.

Moratoriums

A moratorium is a temporary suspension of payments due on a debt. Many creditors are willing to grant full or partial moratoriums for a period usually ranging from three to six months. You need to be familiar with the concepts and specific procedures of repayment before you can employ moratoriums effectively in your recovery. Moratoriums are discussed in detail in Chapter 17. Here, it's important only to know that they exist and that you can use them as part of your overall plan in the stabilizing phase of this program.

Increasing Income

Increasing your income is often a good idea. Does that sound like a ridiculous thing to say?

It isn't. True satisfaction in life rarely comes from money itself. It's nearly always the other way around; money results from satisfaction, or the fact that you enjoy and take pleasure from your life, or however else you wish to describe it.

Here is a truth:

Jim makes $40,000 a year, but consistently spends $45,000, borrowing and going ever deeper into debt, for all the reasons discussed in the earlier chapters. His debts are a constant source of pressure, pain, and unhappiness. If his salary jumps to $80,000 next year, he will almost inevitably begin to spend $90,000, borrowing and going ever deeper into debt. The behavior patterns that resulted from his distorted attitudes about money and self, which led him into debt in the first place, are still wholly intact. He will continue to incur debt, and the pressure, pain, and unhappiness this brought him will still be there. All that will change are the numbers.

So an increase in income is not in itself a solution to debt. Nor, in many cases, is it even necessary. Quite a few people can liberate themselves without a major increase in income simply by adhering to the guidelines already given, and those to come.

This is not to say that such an increase isn't desirable. On the contrary, I and practically everyone else I know who works the Back to the Black program find it very desirable. After all, this is—as has been stated—a program of prosperity and abundance, and money is definitely a part of that. But the point is that, except in the case of chronic underearners, many people can free themselves from debt without a major rise in income. How much *more* you wish to bring into your life is entirely up to you.

Since this is a book about debt, not income, we're not going to deal with increasing your income in specific detail—that is, procedures for successfully switching careers, and the like. However, many of the concepts and techniques in the Back to the Black program can be used to powerful effect toward increasing income, and if you apply them thus they will bring you substantial results.

Do It Again

This is not to be taken as latitude, but . . .

Okay, you thought that *this* situation (an eviction notice, emergency car repair, whatever it was) was impossible. You thought you *had* to debt. Or your brother *forced* the loan on you. Or you simply went nuts and charged $800 worth of clothes (which you couldn't have if you'd canceled your credit card).

Oh God!

You're obliterated by guilt, overwhelmed with remorse, plunged into despair. All the progress you've made has been destroyed. You're hopeless. The program doesn't work. You'll never get out of debt.

Yes, you will.

You didn't really *have* to debt, you know. Not really.

But change isn't always easy. This program is tough sometimes. And old attitudes, old behaviors die hard.

You're not the first to debt in this program, and you sure won't be the last. Maybe as many as a quarter of all those who've succeeded at it debted again themselves somewhere along the line, especially in the early stages. An ancient Chinese proverb says: There's no fault in falling down—the fault lies in not getting up.

So you screwed up. The world didn't end.

Start over again. It happens, but it doesn't *have* to happen. Just for today, this one day, don't incur any new debt. And this time, go straight through to freedom.

PART III

TURNING
IT
AROUND

13

A NEW MODE

As may be apparent already, what we're after in this program is nothing less than a major shift in consciousness—in the attitudes, beliefs, and ideas you have about yourself and your money. This can be the single most important factor in improving the quality of your life and in determining the ease and comfort with which you liberate yourself from debt.

You can succeed without such a shift. If you use nothing but the practical techniques and strategies in this book, you'll *still* bring your debting to a halt and eventually pay off all your creditors, but without a shift in consciousness you'll have a harder time of it, you'll deprive yourself of a great deal of emotional and material gain, and you may well get into trouble again later.

Real fixes take place from within, not from without. Nothing external—from stardom to a winning lottery ticket—is going to make your *self* any better. The self is an internal image, who you perceive yourself to be, a composite of your thoughts and beliefs. If that self doesn't change, then you will continue to act and feel just as you did before; and in time, regardless of circumstances, you will produce exactly the same results you did before; in this context, a decline into debt.

The major part of our reality is created by what we *think*.

Henry Ford said, "If a man tells you he can or cannot do a job, he's right."

The Book of Proverbs says, "For as [a man] thinketh in his heart, so is he."

If I had thought back in the mid-1980s, "There's no point writing a book about debt. No one will ever buy it," then I wouldn't have written this book. And since I wouldn't have written it, none of the hundreds of thousands of people who have bought it over the years would have bought it. My thought would have created my reality.

If you think, "I can't change my consciousness," then you won't change it. And once again, what you *think*—your perceptions and attitudes—will have created your reality.

The material in Part III is primarily conceptual. All the concepts in this book are developmental; they support and enlarge each other. The more you reflect upon them, the deeper the levels of meaning you'll discover in them. And as you integrate them into your consciousness and develop the habit of bringing them to mind, a steady flow of new possibilities will become a regular part of your life.

Taking Action

You can't create a result without taking an action. Wishing never made anything so.

"I'd like to get out of debt."

"I'd like to have more money."

"I'd like to take a vacation."

Of course you would. So would everyone else. The difference between those who get what they wish for and those who don't is action. Nothing happens without it, no matter how powerful your wish. Obvious? Maybe. But frequently overlooked. Let's drive the truth of this home.

Close your eyes. Now, wish very hard for a bag of gold to appear on your doorstep. Wish with all your might. Wish as intensely as you can, as long as you can. Give it everything you've got. Pour it on. Wish! Wish!

Now open your eyes. Go to your doorstep. Is there a bag of gold there?

As a young man, I wished very much to be published. But I needed, when I was nineteen, to take the action of putting a story in an envelope and mailing it to a magazine before I could make my first sale and be published. Which I did, and was.

I needed to take an action.

Donna, a hairstylist, wished she had more money to spend on personal pleasure and for debt repayment. She languished thus for nearly a year, growing ever more frustrated. What she needed was to take action, to have business cards printed, to carry some with her at all times, and to give one to anyone she met who expressed interest. She did, and within six months her income rose 20 percent.

Steve, a professor of philosophy, wished he had a larger apartment, but couldn't afford one. He needed to take the action of developing a syllabus (for a self-awareness seminar), the action of mailing out fliers, the action of advertising, which he did. For the past two years he's been teaching a seminar one weekend each month. This has brought him an additional $19,000 a year, substantially more than he needs to cover the rent on the new apartment in which he now lives.

Taking action is what made the difference in these cases, what always makes the difference. Does that mean taking action always works? No, not at all. Some actions are more effective than others; some end up dead in the water. The point is, you can't get results without them.

Fish lay thousands of eggs. Only a tiny percentage of these ever hatch—yet there are a lot of fish around.

If I take ten actions and only three work, I've still made three gains I couldn't have if I'd simply sat around wishing something were different. It's *taking action* that counts.

You've already taken several yourself:

- You bought this book.
- You're reading it.
- You're keeping a Spending Record.
- You've made a Spending Plan.
- You've drawn up lists to reveal new options to yourself.
- You haven't gone any further into debt, one day at a time.

Those are significant and important actions.

Here's a sampling of the kind of actions others have taken. The nature of the action is less important here than the fact that action was taken. In Chapter 20 we'll discuss ways to target actions to specific goals.

- Surveyed the want ads
- Asked for a raise
- Advertised
- Changed agent
- Made lists
- Finished college degree
- Made cold sales calls
- Bought new business wardrobe
- Scheduled job interviews
- Turned hobby into a profession
- Acquired voice mail service
- Joined professional associations
- Discharged unproductive employees
- Bought new tools and equipment
- Went to bed earlier
- Took a vacation

- Created a website
- Hired accountant
- Telephoned rather than sent letter
- Appeared in person rather than telephoned
- Meditated regularly
- Discussed personal financial situation with someone supportive
- Followed up all inquiries
- Abandoned projects that clearly weren't going to work
- Raised fees
- Changed hairstyle
- Created mailing list
- Consulted with professionals
- Willingly admitted a mistake and changed course
- Created new and up-to-date address book
- Repainted office
- Curtailed workaholism
- Kept accurate records
- Balanced checkbook
- Got rid of old, unnecessary files
- Had fun

Whatever the action is, it's the action that brings about a result, not a wish.

To Hell With the Results

Every action you take is a complete success, regardless of the results. In fact, the results don't matter at all. This may be difficult to grasp at first. Why bother, if the results don't matter? Because there can't be any results if you don't.

A contradiction? Only on the surface. Let's divide this idea of action-and-result into two parts: the part that is mine, and the part that is not—or, the part that I can control, and the part that I can't.

Here's an action: I spend the morning developing an idea for a magazine article, type up a proposal, and send it off to an editor. That is an action I can take, that part is mine. What happens afterward—the result—is totally beyond my control. The editor may give me the assignment. She may ask me to rework the idea and submit it again. She may reject it but ask me to submit others. Or she may reject it without comment.

I have no control over the result. It is out of my hands. It is in the hands of others. All I can control in this situation is the action. The only part that is mine, that is ever mine, is to *take* the action. I can neither dictate nor control the result of any action I take.

I've written many books over the years. Some were immensely popular, some sold only modestly. In each case, I was largely powerless over what happened to them after I took the action of writing them.

They were widely distributed by the publisher, or they were not. A reviewer liked a title, or did not. Potential readers learned of the book, or they did not. Those who did either bought the book, or did not. Those were all results beyond my control.

It is vital to understand this separation of action from result. Since you are powerless over the results, since you can *never* control them, you are liberated from ever having to worry or become anxious about them again.

This is no small thing. It is the very concern over results—usually played out in an imagined negative scenario—that inhibits most of us from taking action in the first place. (Why bother asking her, she'd never go out with me anyway.) Thus, paradoxically, we eliminate any possibility of a positive result because of our fear of a negative result; we never achieve what we desire because we don't take the action that might turn that desire into reality.

Most of us short-circuit several ideas for action each day. An idea pops into mind, we grow excited for an instant, then we're overwhelmed by negative chatter—"Oh that would never work . . . That's not me . . . I'd look like a fool . . . It's hopeless . . . I'm not qualified . . . No one can make money that way." The idea quickly slips away, we do nothing, and continue to languish, yearning for a life we don't have and wishing things were different.

Once you recognize that you can't control or even *influence* the results of your actions, the inhibiting negative chatter will begin to lose its power. Once you begin to understand that the only real point, ever, of taking an action is simply to take it, then you can and will begin to do so.

Fix this in mind:

Each Action You Take Is a Total Success.

You cannot fail when you take an action—because the only thing you wish to accomplish is to take that action. When you do, you have accomplished your goal. What eventually results from the action is irrelevant. You took the action. You were completely successful.

Don't confuse a goal with an action. Donna, the hairstylist, wanted more money to spend on personal pleasure and for debt repayment. That was a goal, not an action. To achieve it, she took a series of separate and independent actions, one at a time, each complete within itself. She didn't concern herself with anything but the single action of the moment; and with each, she considered herself completely successful simply because she took it.

Her actions were:

1. To design and write out the wording of a business card
2. To order the cards printed
3. To carry cards with her every day
4. To give a card to each person she met who seemed a potential client

She didn't succumb to her negative chatter—"This will never work, I'll look too pushy, I'll be too embarrassed to pass out business cards"—and she took each action for its own sake, letting go of the results at each step. Because of that, paradoxically, she did in fact accomplish what she had wanted in the first place—a large increase in income.

- Action is what accomplishes, not wishing.
- You always succeed when you take an action, since the action itself is your success.
- The results of any action you take are utterly beyond your power to control.

So let go of the results. Take the action.

Serenity

To be serene is to be calm and tranquil, to be free of fear and to feel a sense of well-being. Serenity is a desirable state in its own right. It is also a powerful tool in the process of liberating yourself from debt. The closer you come to it, the more effectively you'll function in your financial affairs.

Three excellent ways to cultivate serenity are physical exercise, meditation, and prayer.

The mutual influence between mind and body has been known for centuries. Regular physical exercise provides you with energy, mental clarity, and a positive emotional state. It enhances your ability to relax and to sleep soundly.

Meditation, which comes in a variety of forms, is a mental discipline that enables you to become still, to become utterly quiet in mind and body. It is an ancient and time-honored practice. Over the past several decades, Western medical researchers have repeatedly documented its many positive physiological, intellectual, and emotional benefits.

Prayer has also been recognized for centuries for the support, strength, and comfort it lends to those who undertake it. It requires no specific form or creed. Anything addressed as a prayer, to any form of higher power, *is* a prayer and offers these benefits. "The function of prayer," wrote Kierkegaard, "is not to influence God, but rather to change the nature of the one who prays."

Keep It Simple

Don't complicate things. Keep any task, action, or issue in perspective. See it for what it actually is. Do not assign significance or consequences to it that in itself it does not have.

A letter from a creditor is just that—one letter from one creditor, and nothing more. It's not a judgment on your entire life. It doesn't mean your children won't go to school. It isn't related in any way to your other creditors or your years of debting.

A job interview is just that—a job interview. It's not the make-or-break point of your life. It won't determine your fate. It has nothing to do with any other interview you've ever had.

If, when you tied your shoes in the morning, you were thinking about every pair of shoes you'd ever owned, all the pairs you will own in the future, the repair, maintenance, total cost of a lifetime of shoes, the matching of them to clothes, the running you've done in them and will do in them, the parties you've gone to and will go to in them, and all the rest, you'd drive yourself crazy with the enormity and significance of it—when all you're really doing is tying your shoes.

When you start to grow agitated over a task or a situation, stop. Take a couple of deep breaths. Recognize that what you've probably begun to do is attach a whole baggage train of significance and consequences to it. Uncouple that baggage train and keep it simple. Let the task or situation be its own separate self. Reduce it to what it actually is.

Easy Does It

Worry and fret never swayed a single decision in your favor or paid off a penny of your debt. Neither did fear, despair, or raking yourself over the coals. All they've ever done is make you unhappier. So what's the point?

Go to a movie. Have dinner with a friend. Listen to music. Read a book. Enjoy yourself.

Impossible, you say. I *need* to worry. I need to experience terror. I need to beat myself up.

Okay. Maybe you can give that up in time. But for now, since you're going to do it anyway, let's not leave it to chance and random circumstance. Let's formalize it, let's do it right.

Pick a time. For some reason, people who do this seem to favor 11:45 A.M. or 3:30 P.M. Maybe so it doesn't interfere with lunch or the rest of the day.

Give it five minutes. Five *real* minutes. Don't shirk or use halfway measures—this is serious stuff. We're going to bury you at the bottom of the dungheap of the universe.

Okay? Get ready. Take a deep breath; we want to put a lot of energy into this. Now . . . Go!

Weep and wail. Shudder with fear. Convulse with terror. Moan with despair. That's it! Tear yourself apart. Scream at yourself. Tell yourself what a worthless, sniveling, weak-willed, crummy, rotten piece of human junk you are. Pour it on! Quake with helplessness. Cry out in the face of doom. Heap ashes and dust upon your head. Grovel. Shriek. Condemn. Kick the living daylights out of yourself!

All done?

Good. You have now fulfilled all your moral and ethical obligations to suffer. You can return to your day again and finish it in a humane and happy fashion.

If you really wish to suffer, or think you ought to, then conduct it in this fashion from here on. Five minutes a day, at a regularly appointed hour. For the rest of the time, be good to yourself—relax, play, do what you enjoy doing.

Show Up

To show up, on one level, means to be responsible, to get where you're supposed to be—a job, studio, business appointment—when you're supposed to and to be fully present while you're there, to be prepared and focused. It means entering a record of your checks into your ledger. It means following through on what you said you would.

This isn't being responsible to others, it's being responsible to yourself. That others might benefit from it too is incidental; you're the one who reaps the biggest gains. Your confidence and self-esteem will rise, more money will come in to you, and you'll take increasing control over your own life.

But that's only the business and financial part of showing up—the rest is much larger. It means showing up for your life in general, engaging with it on every level: in romance, family, friends, work, hobbies, sports, recreation, and play. It means taking good care of yourself physically, mentally, and spiritually. This kind of engagement across the spectrum of your life leads automatically to a larger sense of well-being and increased earnings.

Act As If

Everyone experiences fear. Courage is nothing more than following through on an action despite that fear.

In any given situation, act *as if* you weren't afraid, *as if* you didn't doubt yourself. As if you didn't have to blow the project, as if you *were* the best candidate for the job.

Helen is an actress. Despite some early success, a series of defeats and lost roles had undermined her confidence, which had never been more than tentative. She hadn't worked at her craft in nearly four years, though she doggedly continued to go to auditions, taking temporary jobs to support herself. Sometimes she got a callback, but never a part.

"I always screw up the auditions," she said. "I *have* to. I watch myself destroying them, but I can't stop myself."

Helen had experienced a hurtful childhood which had left her feeling worthless and incapable. She understood the dynamics of what had happened to her, but that didn't help much; she still felt powerless over what she perceived as a deep-seated need to sabotage herself.

Someone suggested that she try acting *as if* she didn't have to screw up. At first she was angry. She couldn't believe there could be such a simple answer to a problem that was so deeply embedded. She thought that a solution, if indeed there was a solution, would have to be equally as complicated, equally as painful, and would require several years of work. But she tried it anyway, and at each audition, to the best of her ability, she acted *as if* she didn't have to undermine herself.

She didn't master the technique immediately. Very few do. But she got progressively better at it, and began to pick up small parts and day-work. Then she was hired for a month-long run in a theater in Washington, a small film role, then a six-week run in a theater in New Haven. Now, some two years later, she's working regularly at her craft. She's still not fully convinced that she doesn't have to sabotage herself, but when she begins to feel she's compelled to, she immediately reverts to acting *as if* she doesn't.

Frequently, we are who we pretend to be. In time, if you observe the external practices—act *as if*—then belief will overcome your own doubts.

It's much easier to act your way into constructive thinking than it is to think your way into constructive action.

14

COMRADES IN ARMS

The Back to the Black program in itself, if you adhere to it, will enable you to free yourself from debt regardless of your circumstances. But some people may find it easier and more effective to practice in the context of a support group, in the company of others who have a similar commitment.

Even the Lone Ranger Had Tonto

People in trouble with debt often feel a keen sense of isolation. They speak to no one about it, they feel cut off and alone. This is painful in itself and leads to a sense of hopelessness.

A support group is a powerful tool. It provides access to a large body of experience, strength, and hope that would not otherwise be available. It offers encouragement, a feeling of community, a healthy perspective on distorted attitudes and perceptions, and a sharing of ideas, information, and techniques. At first, many balk at the idea of joining such a group. Pride comes into play, embarrassment, shame, anger.

"I'm not weak," you might say. "I can do it by myself."

Yes, you can. In fact, you'll have to. No one else could even if they wanted to. A support group offers you help, but *you're* the one who has to do the job. Joining a group is not a sign of weakness—just the opposite: It manifests courage and strength, since it flies right in the face of fear and pride, and it is an act of commitment to yourself.

"I don't want to be told what to do."

There are no authority figures in a good support group. It is a community of equals who have come together to solve their common problem and who simply share their experience, strength, and hope with each other.

"I'd be too afraid. I could never talk about this."

That is both a result and a cause of your debt problem. Continued isolation only intensifies it. No one ever walked into a support group eager to begin talking about his situation or without apprehension and reluctance. At first, many simply listen. In time, most begin to speak. Inevitably they find it a relief.

"I'd be humiliated if I ran into someone I know."

Why? Everyone is there for precisely the same reason. They are no different from you, or you from them. Your imagined embarrassment stems from the belief that you've done something wrong, that you're weak-willed or incapable. That belief itself is part of the problem.

Debtors Anonymous

Debtors Anonymous (DA) is the best and most effective support group there is. Its members have dealt directly and successfully with this problem for nearly three decades now. It is a self-help organization that has no dues or fees, with each chapter functioning independently but linked together with the others through the organization's general administrative arm.

The following is more or less representative of a typical meeting:

It's a Friday night. Some fifty people are sitting in molded plastic chairs in a one-room brick building that is part of a church complex in Greenwich Village. It's a comfortable, sparsely furnished room, used by various community groups. Two ceiling fans turn slowly. The group is listening to a woman talk about her life, and about her money.

At each meeting, one member serves as principal speaker. Tonight it's Ruth, who's been a member for three years. She's in her fifties, a commercial artist. She wears a tailored skirt and a long-sleeved beige blouse.

"My family was extremely money oriented," she says. "I grew up thinking it was the paramount value. I was in awe of wealth. I always tried to give the impression that I had money and to live up to the level of my affluent friends."

Her audience is about evenly divided between men and women, early twenties through late sixties and dressed in everything from jeans and sneakers to expensive ensembles and business suits. Most pay close attention to her. Some are distracted by matters they want to bring up later.

Ruth describes a life in which there was never enough. "I *lusted* after money," she says. "I was arrogant and overbearing when I had it. I was totally miserable when I didn't. I always needed more. And I used bank loans and charge cards to get it. I was constantly in debt."

She was adroit at juggling her finances and managed to keep the system going for years, she tells them. But she was living on the edge, feeling ever more pressured, ever more desperate. Finally, it all collapsed.

"I was wiped out," she says. "Everything I had was gone. When I came into the program, I was hysterical. I was stunned. I was suicidal. I couldn't function."

Tonight, three years later, she's relaxed as she tells her story, breaking into laughter several times. She is no longer in debt. Her business is thriving. She concludes, then opens the remaining hour to general discussion.

A public relations man says he understands her earlier despair. He was $73,000 in debt and felt crushed and hopeless when he first came to DA, two and a half years ago. "I never understood money, or what I did with it," he says. He has since paid off $26,000 of his debts, and his marriage, which had been strained by debt, is much stronger.

A physical therapist in her early thirties expresses her pleasure in having watched Ruth change over the last three years. It was months, she says, before she first saw her smile.

A young man in a sweatshirt with the sleeves cut off talks about his fear of asking his employer for a raise. "I know better. I'm learning. But deep down inside I still don't believe I'm worth more money."

A woman in her late twenties is clearly uncomfortable. She finds it nearly incomprehensible, she says, that Ruth and others can cite specific amounts of income and debt so casually. She's been in DA five months, but still hasn't been able to talk in anything but generalities. She wants to tell them now exactly what she does and how much debt she's carrying. She has to force the words out. She works in computer art, she says. She owes $40,000. She is shaken, but also appears relieved. Another woman gives her hand a squeeze.

A man with his temples going gray recounts a meeting with an officer of the bank that is his major creditor. Acting on suggestions given him here, he successfully negotiated a six-month moratorium on payments.

A woman in her mid-twenties suddenly explodes. She's a secretary, and this is only her fourth meeting. "I'm furious," she tells them in a taut, quivering voice. "I hate being in debt! I hate not having enough! I hate everything about this!"

"That's odd," someone else says, deadpan. "The rest of us really loved it."

Several people break into laughter. The secretary glares at them. Then, suddenly, she laughs too.

At the meeting's end, people help put the chairs away and straighten the room. They leave slowly, milling about, breaking into smaller groups to talk or to head out for coffee or food. . . .

Though Debtors Anonymous is well established and growing each year, it is not yet functioning in all parts of the country. If it's not available in your area, you might consider founding a chapter there. The program will help you. Write to:

Debtors Anonymous, General Service Office
P.O. Box 920888
Needham, MA 02492-0009

email: da-gso@mindspring.com
Telephone: 781-453-2743
www.debtorsanonymous.org

OR . . .

Alternatively, you may want to put together a support group of your own. If so, begin by discreetly seeking out others with a debt problem. You can find them through a trusted friend, your therapist, your doctor or cleric, through other self-help programs, or similar avenues.

Schedule a weekly meeting of an hour or an hour and a half together. Use the material in this book as subject matter for discussion. Share your experiences, your difficulties and successes with each other.

It may seem awkward at first, but you'll feel easier as time passes—and you'll find that it's of tremendous value.

15

THROUGH A GLASS, CLEARLY

enturies ago the manufacturing process of glass was crude and the glass produced was darkish and of uneven surface—it permitted only a small quantity of light to pass, and what could be seen through it was murky and distorted. Thus the Biblical phrase "to see through a glass, darkly."

The concepts in this chapter are intended to help correct that, to help you see certain aspects of your life through a glass, clearly.

You Don't <u>Have</u> to Do Anything

When people under pressure from debt think of something they'd like to do, or to have, their next thought—almost instantaneous—is frequently: "I can't afford that." This is depressing, and leads to living with a constant sense of impoverishment and restriction, which generally leads to further debting.

You can afford much more than you think you can. In truth, there's nothing that you *have* to do with your money.

For the most part, it's not that you can't afford something, but rather that you choose to spend the money in other ways.

You *choose* to pay your rent. You *choose* to pay your telephone bill.

"But I *need* this much space."

"But I *have* to have a telephone."

Untrue.

Sure, reduced living quarters could be less pleasant and might even pose problems. And things would certainly be more inconvenient without a telephone, even difficult and impractical. But neither a large apartment nor a wireless number-memory telephone with call-waiting service and voice mail are essential to the maintenance of life. What you *need* are food, shelter, and clothing—what *kind,* and everything beyond your basic needs, are choices.

I don't by any means advocate a life stripped down to bare survival requirements. That's counterproductive and only magnifies a debt problem. But I do want to stress the value of recognizing that you have a large number of options with your money right now, today.

Early in my own recovery, when I was still living right at the zero point—meeting my expenses each month, but not knowing how I was going to do it next month—something popped in the picture tube of my television and nearly all the color washed out, leaving the hues weak and pale. I enjoy watching movies on videocassette. It contributes to my sense of well-being and pleasure in life.

The repair was estimated at $225. I couldn't *afford* that. It was yet one more thing, among so many, that I couldn't—yet another diminution of my life, another stripping away from me. At least that's how I saw it.

Ed, the man who'd spoken to me about the dental work, about the need to start spending on myself, asked me how much I had at the moment.

"About $1,500," I said. "But I need that for rent, medical insurance, bills. It's all earmarked."

"But the fact remains," he said, "that you do have enough to get your television repaired, more than enough. You *can* afford it. You're *choosing* to do other things with the money."

It wasn't sophistry. He was right.

I *was* choosing to pay my rent, my health insurance. I was choosing to meet my debt repayment schedule. I was choosing, I had to recognize when I looked at my Spending Plan, to spend money on clothes this month, on entertainment, on dining out. But years of living with mounting debt had clouded my vision of that fact, if indeed I'd ever seen it clearly. My instinctive response and my belief was, I can't *afford* that.

An editor I knew several years ago was always bemoaning the many things he couldn't afford, from a new business suit to a ski weekend. He believed he couldn't afford these, and it depressed him. Yet he could afford to dine out three times a week and take a cab to and from work every day.

Once you recognize that you always have choices in the ways you spend your money, that you are constantly choosing, you'll begin to make more pleasing and satisfying choices. And the feeling that you can rarely afford to do or have the things that you want will begin to fall away from you—as is fitting, since it's largely a misperception.

"Oh yeah? Well, what I want is a six-month cruise around the world. You gonna tell me I can afford that?"

If that's what you truly want—if it's not simply a vague yearning or fanciful whim—then you probably can. If you deeply desire it, then eventually you'll find a way to shift your money around and to bring more in, to the point where you can make that choice.

There's very little that you *have* to do with your money. It's mostly a matter of what you *choose* to do with it.

Look at That!

We've pointed out that when you come to focus obsessively on your debts it's as if a filter is placed over your eyes, blocking out the sight of all that is good in your life and all that you actually do have. Your debts become exaggerated and monstrous. You can see only lack and deprivation. Here is a simple but effective way to begin to reverse this, to expose that perception for the distortion it really is.

Sit down with a pad of paper. Across the top write, *Things in My Life for Which I Am Grateful.* Or, *Things in My Life I Appreciate and Enjoy.*

Now list everything you can think of.

Some people nearly gag over this idea. "How can I do that when I'm in so much pain, when there's so much I've lost, when there's so much I don't have, when everyone else has so much more than I do!"

That's the point. All you can see is your suffering and what you don't have. You've become blind to what you *do* have.

Once I lived in a fourteen-room house on a seven-acre wooded estate with a swimming pool, guest cottages, and a large studio building that overlooked a meadow, with a view of the mountain behind. When I began my recovery I was living in a small studio apartment in the city.

All that I could see then was what I'd lost, what I didn't have, how impoverished and hopeless my life was.

Among other things to which I was blind was the fact that my apartment had been newly renovated in an aesthetically pleasing way, that it was located in a hundred-year-old federal building in a pleasant neighborhood, that it possessed a handsome fieldstone fireplace, that I had beautiful fruit-wood blinds, that there was excellent ventilation, that it overlooked a peaceful courtyard with trees and gardens, that my neighbors were civil and quiet . . . and much, much more.

To say that you're too worried and depressed over your debts to make such a list, that you'll have to wait until you feel better, is to put the cart before the horse. It's making the list that will help to improve your emotions, to clear your vision and, as a consequence, begin to improve the quality of your entire life.

Some of the things a gratitude list might include are:

- I'm healthy
- My kids are great
- My stereo
- My dog
- I play a great game of tennis
- My husband loves me
- Job
- My library
- The house
- I'm good-looking
- My friends
- My computer
- The high ceilings in the apartment
- My video camera
- My gun collection
- The health club
- The oak tree
- My firm mattress
- My lover
- My jewelry
- The dishwasher
- The camping gear
- I dance well
- The antique ice-cream table
- My answering machine

Write out a new list every three months or so for the first year. Afterwards, every five or six months. It helps you keep the idea of lack and deprivation where it belongs—on the scrap heap.

Fieldstripping Your Vocabulary

"I'm under pressure," you say.

"I'm up against the wall."

"Everything's closing in on me."

"I'm going under."

"I can't hold out."

Your subconscious hears this. It believes you. It goes crazy: "Oh God, we're under attack! We're going to die! It's hopeless! We're lost. What are we going to *do*?"

Your emotions respond accordingly; you become panicky or depressed. And why not? You're under pressure, you're up against the wall, everything's closing in on you, you're going under and can't hold out.

Who wouldn't feel terrible about that?

But that's not what's happening.

What is happening is that you've felt under siege for so long that by reflex you answer nearly every inquiry about how you're doing with an image of struggle. Your subconscious, however, doesn't know that. It believes what you're saying—and dutifully supplies you with all the emotions appropriate to imminent catastrophe.

When you use the language of strife, of hardship and calamity, you create a destructive emotional climate within yourself and reinforce a negative consciousness.

Strip this language and imagery out of your vocabulary. Don't talk struggle. Don't talk lack and deprivation. Don't create those situations by giving voice to them.

Remember that your feelings aren't facts. Don't fuel them this way. You'll only convince yourself and others that they're true and thereby invite negative events.

Today, right now, you are perfectly all right. You've

stopped your debt-spiral cold. You're taking increasing control of your life. You're bringing in more money. One day at a time, your life is growing progressively better.

I Never Knew I Was This Good

By now it's clear that most of our emotions and behavior are dictated by what we believe, by what we *think* to be true. These beliefs operate largely in our subconscious.

How did we acquire them?

Basically, we were programmed, by ourselves and others. Most of this programming took place when we were quite young—before our intelligence was sufficiently developed to be of much help to us in evaluating what was coming in. It happened in three different ways:

1. We processed various bits of information about ourselves and the world and drew a conclusion.
2. Someone told us something about ourselves or the world and we accepted it as true.
3. We overheard others talking about us or the world and we believed what they said.

So early on, before we could even begin to understand what such statements meant, we accepted such distortions as:

"Life is tough."

"I'm not worth much."

"Money is evil."

"You have to suffer to get ahead."

"It's immoral to have things when others are starving."

And all the rest.

We then proceeded to feel, live, and behave according to these beliefs—which were not a set of universal truths, but

simply the distorted judgments and opinions of others programmed into our subconscious.

This negative programming has a crippling and destructive effect upon us. We need to counteract it. One of the
most effective ways to do that is to take control of the process
ourselves, through the use of affirmations.

To affirm something is to declare it positively or firmly, to
maintain that it is true. The word derives from the Latin *af-
firmare*, which means to fix in place, to make solid, to make
strong or healthy.

An affirmation is a strong positive thought you implant in
your subconscious with the intention of producing a healthy
change in your attitudes and perceptions. Affirmations are
much more than simple positive thinking—if used in an effective format. Used thus, they become specific and powerful
vehicles of change, and, if systematically employed, can and
do bring about such internal change, which, by consequence,
leads inevitably to external change.

It doesn't matter whether or not you believe your affirmations. Even if you find them absurd and incredible, your
subconscious will in time begin to accept them.

Here is the best way to work with them. Divide a sheet of
paper in half lengthwise by drawing a line down the middle.
Write the positive affirmation on the left. As soon as you do,
jot down on the right the first thought that comes to mind.
This response column is important. It allows your subconscious to raise all the objections it wants, to get the junk out
of its system.

Write the affirmation five times in the first person "I."
Then five times in the second person, using your own name.
Then five times in the third person, using your own name.
Using the three voices—first, second, and third person—gets
this new attitude into your subconscious in the same way the
old distorted ones entered: through what you told yourself,
what others told you, and what you heard others say.

The process looks like this:

I make money very easily.	That's a crock!
I make money very easily.	Blow it out your nose.
I make money very easily.	So does the beggar on the corner.
I make money very easily.	Tell it to the Marines.
I make money very easily.	Yeah, sometimes.
Jerry, you make money very easily.	In a pig's eye.
Jerry, you make money very easily.	Once.
Jerry, you make money very easily.	Your mama.
Jerry, you make money very easily.	Ho-hum.
Jerry, you make money very easily.	What am I, J. Paul Getty?
Jerry makes money very easily.	Sure he does.
Jerry makes money very easily.	Okay, okay, already.
Jerry makes money very easily.	This is boring.
Jerry makes money very easily.	Maybe he does.
Jerry makes money very easily.	Uh-huh.

Here are a few affirmations people have used to strong effect:

- I have everything I need to get everything I want.
- More money comes in to me every day.
- Each day I get further and further out of debt.
- The universe now brings me all the prosperity I need.
- I handle money easily and well.
- Abundance is my true state of being. I am now ready to accept it fully and joyously.
- My success is big, powerful, and irresistible.
- The universe is total abundance.
- I now have more than enough money to satisfy all my needs and desires.
- The more I win, the better I feel about letting others win.
- Money is my friend.
- It's okay for me to exceed my goals.

- The more I prosper, the more I have to share with others.
- I am now ready to accept all the joy and prosperity life has to offer me.

If you had a strong negative reaction to any of these—found them irrational, absurd, even horrifying—then they are precisely the ones you should start working with. A powerful negative response usually means that a given affirmation is colliding head-on with its opposite, with a distorted belief that's deeply entrenched in your subconscious. And those are the ones you most need to root out.

It's best to work with a single affirmation at a time. Write it out in the style just given twice each day for ten to fourteen days. Be sure to use the response column. (You'll probably note that the negative responses become less violent after a few days and that some tentative positive ones begin to creep in. That's a sign that your subconscious is beginning to give up the ferocity of its initial resistance.) Write it out one final day without the response column, allowing it to sink in uncontested. Then take two or three days off, after which you can begin the process over with a new affirmation.

You can create your own affirmations too, tailoring them to specific needs. First, identify the negative statement. For example: "I always get nervous and flustered when demands are placed on me." Then reverse it into its opposite, being careful to use only positive language; don't phrase it in a way that *seems* positive but that in fact contains either a negative subtext or invites negative association. "I never get nervous or flustered when demands are placed on me" isn't very helpful. It contains negative words and elements of struggle and denial.

Let's try again.

Negative statement: "I always get nervous and flustered when demands are placed on me."

Affirmation: "Challenges always bring out the best in me." Or: "The more others ask of me, the happier and more confident I become."

Remember, your initial disbelief or even revulsion toward the affirmation is irrelevant to its eventual impact. If you work with it, it will begin to work for you. You can strengthen the process by taking a few moments after waking and at intervals during the day to simply say the affirmation out loud or silently to yourself three or four times.

Many scoff when they first encounter the idea of affirmations. So did I. But on the other hand, I eventually decided, a closed mind has never been the hallmark of a functioning intelligence, and it wouldn't cost me much to give it a try. So I did. Carefully, privately—after all, I had a reputation of intellectual skepticism to maintain. For several years I employed affirmations regularly; I'm enough of a pragmatist to use what works.

What the Bacon Looks Like

It's a lot easier to bring home the bacon when you know what the bacon looks like.

Everything that is made or done by man first comes into being in thought. It is then translated into the external world. Nothing—from a relationship to a cabinet or a work of art—can be created without the idea, a picture, an image, or a sense of the thing first occurring in the mind.

An architect first "sees" a building mentally. He then translates what he "sees"—a form of thought—onto paper, which is the design. Blueprints follow, construction crews and tradesmen go to work, and finally a building comes into existence.

Bringing this "seeing"—this thought process—under

conscious control and using it in a deliberate, systematic way to gain something you wish to possess or accomplish is called *visualization*.

Visualization is a potent tool. Psychology, theoretical physics, and metaphysics all document its effectiveness and offer reasoned theories as to why it works. The why is moot, so far as our purposes go; what's important here is *that* it works.

The technique is simple and remains the same whether you wish to acquire an object, succeed at a project, or effect a change in your internal or external life.

Let's say, for example, that what you want is a dining room table.

Sit in a comfortable chair or lie on the floor, whichever seems most natural. Close your eyes, breathe deeply, and consciously relax your body, part by part, just as you would while preparing to meditate or undertake a deep relaxation exercise. Let your mind become as clear and still as you can.

Form a mental picture of the table you would like to have. *See yourself already in possession of it.* See its shape, its color. See the way the light glances off it. See it in your home, against the background of your other furniture. See yourself enjoying it. See yourself polishing it, setting a vase of flowers on it. See yourself serving dinner on it, lounging around it over coffee with guests. See it in your life, right now, and see yourself enjoying and taking pleasure from it, in as many ways and in as much detail as you can.

Bring as strong a sense of reality to these images as you can. See the table not as something you want, that you hope will come to you, but as something that is present in your life right now, that you already have. It is real. It is yours.

Concentrate on the visualization, but don't work at it, don't struggle. Stay relaxed. Take pleasure from it. Five minutes of this, or however long is comfortable for you, is enough. When you feel the visualization is complete, end it with a silent affirmation.

An effective one is:

> ***This or Something Better***
> ***Now Enters My Life***
> ***in a Totally Satisfying and***
> ***Harmonious Way,***
> ***and I Appreciate It***
> ***and Am Pleased by It.***

That's all there is to it.

Visualization is easiest in the early morning before you become involved in your day, or in the evening when your tasks are behind you. Do it once or twice a day for a week or so, whatever feels right, concentrating on a single goal. You can also do miniversions of ten or twenty seconds at various times during the day.

In the context of this program, some of the things people have visualized and brought into their lives include:

- Vacation
- Successful work project
- Promotion
- Getting through the day without anger or fear
- Raise
- Job interview
- Car
- Calm negotiation with creditors
- Clothes
- Career change
- Favorable legal decision
- An openness to new ideas
- Increased health
- Better concentration
- Educational degrees

- Skilled advisers
- Income jumps
- Larger living quarters
- The ability to use visualization
- Windfall profits

There are no limitations. Visualization can be applied to anything you want to have, be, or do.

The degree of success you'll have with it depends on three elements:

1. *Desire.* This must be strong. You must truly and intensely want to create whatever it is you're visualizing, not simply wish or vaguely yearn for it. You must be clear and firm.
2. *Belief.* The more conviction you can generate that your goal is truly possible, that you *can* have it, then the more effective visualization will be for you. Uncertainty and doubt will undermine it.
3. *Acceptance.* You must be completely willing to accept whatever you are visualizing, to accept it into your life totally and without reservation. Ambiguity will block the process.

Visualization often produces its results in completely unexpected ways.

The dining room table in our example could manifest itself in any of a variety of ways. A friend might decide to redecorate and ask if you'd like his present table, the one he's replacing. You could receive a raise or bonus that would easily cover buying a table. A sale might bring one down to a price that fits your present Spending Plan. A relative could give you one as an anniversary present. You might be promoted, transferred to another city, and end up in a house instead of an apartment, with a whole new set of furniture, among which a dining room table is but one piece.

The timing is unpredictable too. Sometimes a manifestation occurs so rapidly you might become unnerved. Other times it seems nothing is going to happen at all, you forget about it; then several months or more later it pops into your life.

Visualization—like affirmation—is hard for many people to credit or practice at first; years of negative conditioning and the power of distorted attitudes and perceptions have inhibited these people and made them skeptical and pessimistic. If you have trouble with the concept, the best antidote is simply to begin the practice to the best of your ability.

Start small, with goals that are fairly easy for you to believe are possible. As you gain confidence and become more experienced, you can enlarge your objectives.

PART IV

FREEDOM, PROSPERITY, & ABUNDANCE

16

GETTING OUT:
PART 1

You've made remarkable achievements since you first opened this book. What you've learned about yourself, debt, and your relationship to money, along with the techniques you've begun to practice and the concepts you're absorbing, have already placed you well along the way to freedom from debt. In a sense, this final process isn't much more than a mopping-up operation.

That's not to say that it's a piece of cake. It isn't. You'll run into trouble. You'll probably feel like hell sometimes and want to chuck the whole thing over. Don't. Those are just feelings. You can last them out. Keep going, keep working the program. You'll resolve every problem you encounter, you'll come out on the other side of your emotions.

Remember that hundreds of thousands have gone before you. Like them, you too can and will liberate yourself from debt and go on to live in prosperity and abundance.

A Full Commitment

Establish in yourself a full commitment to repay every dollar you owe. You borrowed it; you have an ethical obligation to pay it back.

Any anger you may feel toward a particular creditor, justified or not, is an issue entirely separate and apart from your debt.

Not only is this commitment "right," it's of large personal value to *you*. It is a cornerstone of your recovery, a manifestation of your self-esteem, your strength, and your confidence in your ability to fulfill all of your own needs and responsibilities.

The Ideal Repayment Plan

A *Repayment Plan* is just that—a plan for paying off your debts.

A crucial point to make here is: *Repayment is not to be made at the expense of the quality of your own life.* That would defeat the central thrust of this program and possibly cause a relapse into new debting.

This is hard for many people to accept. Understandably, they want to rid themselves of what has appeared to be the source of all this stress and unhappiness as quickly as possible. But a vital part of your recovery is to remember that you are *not* living for your creditors, to understand that you have not been sentenced to lack and deprivation. You are committed to repaying each creditor in full, but *you* come first; *they* come second.

It's time to add a new category to your Spending Plan—"Debt Repayment." The amount you can assign to it is irrelevant at this stage, even if it's only $5 a month.

Payments nearly always start small. In fact, many people make none at all—against *any* of their debts—for several months. It is absolutely necessary to stabilize first—to be sure that expenses do not exceed income—and to develop a reasonable Spending Plan, one that takes into account such personal needs as entertainment, health care, and clothing before you even consider beginning to make repayment.

"But that's impossible! My creditors won't wait, and they'd never accept $5 a month!"

Yes they will, if you're being honest. They have little choice. They may not like it, they may insult you and threaten dire consequences. They might even take aggressive action against you. But you will prevail. Even in court, if it goes that far. Which it usually doesn't. So long as you remain honest and stick to your purpose, no one can force you to pay them more than you can actually afford to pay.

Get out your Spending Plan and the complete list of your debts, the one you put together earlier. Find a comfortable chair. Place a calculator, a pad of paper, and a pencil at hand. Relax. Now:

1. Consult your Spending Plan. Determine how much—in total—you could pay toward your debts each month without inflicting lack or deprivation upon yourself. Write that number down. Let's say, for purposes of illustration, that the amount is $100.
2. List all your creditors and the amount you owe each one.
3. Add up your total debt.
4. Use your calculator to determine each creditor's share, or percentage, of the total. This is easy. The formula is: C ÷ T = CP. (Creditor's Amount divided by Total Debt equals Creditor's Percentage.)

For example: You owe your brother $2,000. Your total debt is $15,600. Divide the amount you owe your brother ($2,000) by your total debt ($15,600). The answer equals your brother's share, or percentage, of that total debt.

BROTHER		TOTAL DEBT		BROTHER'S SHARE
$2,000	÷	$15,600	=	.13 or 13%

Do this for each of your creditors. The result might look like this:

TOTAL DEBT: $15,600

CREDITOR			TOTAL		SHARE
Chase Bank	$10,000	÷	$15,600	=	64%
MasterCard	2,400	÷	15,600	=	15
Brother	2,000	÷	15,600	=	13
Judy	1,200	÷	15,600	=	8
			$15,600	=	100%

If a given share comes out to a fraction, round up or down to the nearest percentage point: .166 (or 16.6 percent) would become 17 percent; .164 (or 16.4 percent) would become 16 percent.

This and the following are the only two math formulas in the entire book. Just follow the examples; your calculator will do the actual math for you. If you go blank in the face of them—as some do—don't worry about it. Get a friend to help you; it will only require a couple of minutes.

5. Now multiply each creditor's percentage by the total amount you can pay each month, which you determined in the first step.

To illustrate, let's say the list of creditors in the previous example is your list and that the $100 we cited in Step 1 is the amount you can pay. You want to know how much you can repay your brother each month. To determine this, multiply your brother's share (13 percent) by the total amount you can repay ($100):

BROTHER'S SHARE		TOTAL PAYMENT		BROTHER'S PAYMENT
13%	×	$100	=	$13.00

Follow the same procedure for each of your creditors. The answers tell you what amount you can repay each creditor each month. For example:

TOTAL MONEY AVAILABLE
EACH MONTH FOR REPAYMENT: $100

CREDITORS' SHARE		TOTAL PAYMENT		CREDITORS' PAYMENT
Chase Bank 64%	x	$100	=	$64.00
MasterCard 15	x	100	=	15.00
Parents 13	x	100	=	13.00
Judy 8	x	100	=	8.00
100%			=	$100.00

"But those are chickenfeed numbers; *I'm* $150,000 in debt!"

So what? Some people owe more than you do, some less. The numbers don't matter. The principle remains the same.

"It'll take forever to pay off $15,600 at $100 a month!"

It only seems that way. Payments nearly always start small. They increase as time passes. The process builds on itself; in the end, repayment is often rapid and dramatic.

What matters here is that you have completely reversed your situation. You are now getting *out* of debt instead of *into* debt. That is a stunning achievement.

A Dollar a Month

This point is so important that we're going to make it a separate topic: If all you can reasonably pay toward your debts is $1 a month, then that is enough.

Any embarrassment or discomfort you feel about that stems from false pride, from a fear of what your creditors will think of you, how they might insult or threaten you, and from old distorted attitudes and perceptions.

It is necessary to hold the line here, despite your ego or fear. Creditors may well try to push your buttons. If you capitulate out of anger or dread and agree to pay them more than you can truly afford, you'll begin to live for them again, you'll liable yourself to additional stress, and you may well end up incurring new debt.

That's what happened to Hank, a plumber. His initial Repayment Plan called for a $95 a month against a total debt of $18,000. His former supplier rejected his first attempt to negotiate and threatened to turn his account over to a collection agency. His father-in-law expressed disappointment, his brother contempt. Hank lost sight of his recovery. He wanted to protect his credit rating at all costs, he couldn't bear his father-in-law's implication that he was a failure, he was furious with his brother.

Hank's ego and fear took over. He proved he was responsible, he proved he was capable, he proved he was strong—he proved it on their terms, agreeing to repay $690 each month.

His life became stressful again, a sense of deprivation and looming catastrophe returned. Four months later he was debting again, and this time he fell into a despair deeper than he had ever known before.

Cynthia, a buyer for a large retail store, was $44,000 in debt when she began this program. She came from a privileged background and was haughty, even arrogant. Her first Repayment Plan called for $150 a month. Among her creditors was a dry cleaner to whom she owed $325. His monthly share came out to $1.10, which she increased to $1.50. Though it was a terrible blow to her ego, and not easy for her, she held the line.

"I can't *begin* to tell you how that made me feel," she says. "I didn't think I could bear the humiliation. *I* was a champagne and limousine woman."

At $1.50 a month, it would have taken Cynthia eighteen years to pay off that $325 debt. It didn't. As she continued to refrain from debting and worked this program, she had steadily more money at her disposal. She adjusted her spending and repayment plans accordingly, made her last payment to the dry cleaner nineteen months after she began her repayments, and was completely out of debt, to all of her creditors, in four and a half years.

For now, if all you can pay toward your debts is $1 a month, then that is enough. You've broken the debting cycle. One step at a time, you're moving toward total freedom.

Repayment Plans Aren't Always Ideal

The major values in an ideal—or proportionally balanced—Repayment Plan are:

1. It allows you to make smooth, steady, and calming progress toward full liquidation of your debts.
2. It is fair to all your creditors, since none is being paid off more rapidly than another.
3. It occasionally makes negotiation easier, since some creditors will respond more favorably when they understand that you are not shorting them in favor of others.

But often it's not possible to be proportional. A given creditor might run amok, some interest rates may be punishingly high, the utility company might be on the verge of shutting off your lights.

In such cases you'll probably want to adjust your plan to compensate. But however you modify it, keep two things in mind: *You* come first, your creditors second; and, one day at a time, you don't debt anymore.

The Question of Interest

Where does interest fit into all this?

Ideally the figure for the total amount you can repay

each month includes both interest and principal. But what if it doesn't? What happens if, say, you have a lot of credit card debt and the interest on that alone is $100, $200 a month?

Your first move, as it is with any such question, is to sit down and draw up a list of as many options and possibilities as you can think of. Perhaps you can find a way to cut fat from other categories in your Spending Plan. Maybe you can think of ways to bring in more money. Possibly "Interest Payment" should become a separate category itself; you'd then need to include it with the others in calculating your total expenses for the month.

"Oh hogwash! They're billing me $300 a month in interest alone. I can't meet that no matter how many damn lists I draw up unless I debt somewhere!"

You may be right—the lists might not help you at all. But what makes you think your situation will improve if you incur new debt? It won't. It'll only get worse. Remember: You can not get out of debt by borrowing more money.

So what do you do?

First, forget principal payment altogether.

Second, don't even *think* about slashing the categories that contribute to your enjoyment of life (assuming you've been reasonable there).

Third, if there's no room in your Spending Plan for interest payments, forget about them too.

(For now, anyway. And only if truly essential, if you would have to debt somewhere else otherwise. Unpaid interest compounding against you can be devastating. You want to avoid it if you can. I treated the monthly interest on my own debts as a necessary expense from the first day, as necessary as food and shelter, and paid it each month.)

"I'll die! They'll kill me!"

No they won't. You have other options, which we'll discuss in Chapters 17 and 18.

Insane Interest

A final word on this subject. Interest is one thing; insane interest—or what used to be called usury—is something else. Let's say you owe $2,000 to one of the following. What does this mean to you, in interest payments alone?

- Your father, at a friendly 5 percent—you pay $100 a year in interest.
- Your bank, at 15 percent—you pay $300 a year in interest.
- Your credit card, at 20 percent—you pay $400 a year in interest.
- A loan shark (God forbid), at a standard "$7 for $5 in two weeks." This is a *weekly* rate of 20 percent—you pay $20,800 a year in interest!

In the case of outrageous interest, it's best to adjust your Repayment Plan in a manner that will reduce the principal on that particular debt the most quickly.

Debt Shifting

Debt shifting is one way to relieve pressure or neutralize a high interest rate. The amount of the debt remains the same; you simply transfer it to a new creditor.

For example: Karen, a secretary, had borrowed $800 from her boyfriend. When the relationship ended, her boyfriend was angry, upset, and felt that she'd used him. He demanded full repayment immediately. He wrote letters, left messages on her answering machine. It was emotionally difficult for Karen. A good friend who knew about her recovery program loaned her the $800 so she could pay her ex-boyfriend, and accepted a $65-a-month repayment plan from Karen.

Tony, a chef, borrowed $5,700 from his brother at 5 percent interest in order to pay off the $5,700 he owed on his credit card, which was costing him 19.5 percent interest—a savings of $827 a year in interest charges, or $69 per month.

Irene was four months in arrears to her landlord, for a total of $3,900, and he had begun eviction proceedings. She borrowed the $3,900 from a cousin, paid the landlord in a lump sum, and repaid her cousin at $175 a month.

When you shift a debt, you do *not* incur a new debt. You simply exchange one creditor for another. The debt remains exactly the same. Yesterday you owed $1,500 to Sam, who was making your life miserable. This morning, to alleviate the pressure, you borrowed $1,500 from Jill and paid Sam off. You still owe $1,500. The only difference is that now you owe it to Jill instead of Sam.

Generally this requires a relative or friend who understands your situation and has confidence in your recovery. And of course you can not borrow more from the new creditor than you are paying to the old one. If, for example, you were to borrow $1,750 from Jill, pay Sam off with $1,500, and use the extra $250 to meet current expenses, that would be a new debt—you'd now owe $1,750 instead of $1,500.

In the main, it's better to deal with your existing creditors as they stand. But debt shifting, in a situation of exceptional duress, is a viable option.

Repayment Surplus

Most people discover in the course of their recovery that changed circumstances now allow them to repay more each month than their Repayment Plan calls for. In this happy event there is a temptation—which seems logical at first glance—to begin putting the surplus against your highest-interest debt and pay it off more quickly, thus realizing a savings on interest. Continuing, goes this reasoning, once we liquidate that debt, we'll add the total amount we had been paying on it each month to our payment on the debt with the next highest interest, and so on.

From a strictly financial point of view this makes perfect sense, and would be heartily endorsed by accountants, book-keepers, and financial planners. But we're not accountants, bookkeepers, and financial planners (well, some of us are, actually); and their clients—most of them, anyway—aren't chronic or compulsive debtors who are creating a new way of life.

You can do a little of this piling up against your highest-interest debt if you'd like, especially if all your creditors are satisfied with your existing repayment schedule, but for debtors in recovery, barring insane interest on a particular debt, the proportionally balanced Repayment Plan is best. It's clear, ethical, and a source of self-esteem. It also helps you maintain good relationships with your creditors.

17

Getting Out:
Part 2

You've begun to turn your life around. You feel strong, good, filled with self-esteem.

It's time now to negotiate with your creditors.

Some people panic at this point. There's no reason to. Take a couple of deep breaths. Relax. Consider what you've already done, how far you've come. That panic is erupting out of an old self, out of your former life in which you had little understanding of what was happening to you, in which you were powerless over your increasing debts.

All that has changed. Right now, you know more about yourself and your money than 90 percent of the population do about themselves and their money. You are in control. You *know* what you're doing. That is a source of strength and power.

Honesty

Honesty is essential—with yourself and with your creditors. Without it, there will be no real improvement in your life. Nor are you likely to get out of debt. If you try to "beat" your creditors or use the concepts and techniques in this book in a scheming or manipulative way, you will ultimately only worsen your situation.

This honesty is for *your* benefit.

Hi, It's Me

Hiding from creditors—ignoring their letters, avoiding their phone calls—has a progressively damaging effect:

1. Your fear remains ever present and escalates with each new incident.
2. Your creditors become increasingly angrier and more aggressive.
3. The stress mounts, your financial condition deteriorates.

Take the initiative. Make contact. When *you* get in touch with *them*, you are taking action and establishing a record of good faith.

Set up an appointment if you can. A personal meeting is always the most effective way to deal with a creditor. If that's not possible, use the telephone. If you can't get through by phone, write a letter. But whichever way, take the initiative. Go to them. Don't wait for them to come to you.

Be prepared before you initiate the contact. Have all the facts and figures at hand. *Know* what you're doing.

Explain your situation forthrightly. Your honesty will serve you well here: Since you're not trying to con anyone, since you're not concealing anything, you are not vulnerable; you run no risk of being found out in anything underhanded or scheming.

Tell your creditor that you regret this situation, that you are determined to correct it, and that you are committed to repaying him in full.

Negotiate according to the realities of your Spending and Repayment plans. Remember, they are real. You cannot repay more than you are capable of repaying; and you *know* what that figure is.

If you wish, be candid with your creditor about what happened to you and what you finally came to understand about your situation. Tell him that you have undertaken a financial recovery program. Inform him of your membership in a support group. Show him this book. Share your Spending and Repayment plans with him if you feel that's appropriate or helpful. Some people can't bring themselves to do this. Others can. Those who can have found that it often has a positive effect on their creditors.

Remain steady and calm through all your dealings with your creditor, regardless of his attitudes and behavior. If you don't *feel* steady and calm, *act* so. Reacting or speaking out of anger or fear will only work to your detriment.

"This is all very nice, but do you expect me to believe that they'll all love me and go along with me just because I'm being honest?"

Nope.

Most of your personal creditors—friends, relatives, associates—*will* be appreciative and *will* support you. They loaned you the money in the first place because they cared about you. Most will be relieved and happy to see that you're taking positive action on your own behalf and will be glad to know they'll be getting their money back on a reliable schedule.

Janet, a teacher at a private school, was estranged from her closest friend because of a $4,000 debt. Janet had made a few sporadic payments and many promises she'd never been able to keep. Her friend had eventually become disappointed and impatient with her. Janet reacted with guilt and defensive anger; they hadn't spoken in a year. When Janet formulated a Repayment Plan, she called her friend and made a lunch date. There, she explained her situation and showed her friend her Spending and Repayment plans. Though she could only repay $35 each month, the woman accepted the offer instantly and embraced her, and their relationship became close and satisfying again.

This kind of reconciliation with friends and family is a common experience among people who work this program. Some have made low monthly payments more attractive by offering to pay interest on the outstanding balance equal to or a point above what the creditor would be earning if she had the sum invested in a money-market account.

"That's fine for family and friends, but *my* creditors are institutions. They work with an iron fist."

Sometimes they do—and you may have to take some blows, which we'll discuss in the next chapter. But with surprising frequency, despite occasional threats, they'll respond not with an iron fist, but with a firm, businesslike handshake—now and then, even a touch of warmth.

Miriam, an editor, made contact with Macy's, to whom she owed $1,100. The amount due was $120 per month. She explained her situation to them. They not only granted her an immediate three-month moratorium but followed up with a letter expressing regret that she'd found herself in difficulty.

Ted, a photographic technician, owed a certain department store $485. His monthly payment was $40. He was three months in arrears when he made contact with them. They were flabbergasted. He was unique in their experience, they said. No one else had ever called to express regret, state a commitment to pay, explain his problem, and ask for their cooperation in working out a solution. They accepted a beginning schedule of $10 per month from him.

Ted called each month to keep them abreast of his situation. When the store closed as a business, its overdue accounts were turned over to a collection agency. Ted immediately got in touch with the lawyer heading the agency. She was equally startled by his initiative. At that point, Ted's discretionary income was rising. She agreed to accept $20 per month. Ted maintained monthly contact with her, eventually raised his payment to $30, then $40, and liquidated the debt.

Even when an institutional creditor refuses discussion and demands what's due according to the original agreement, it may still come around later if you remain persistent. The first person with whom you speak is probably a lower-level employee who has no authority to make a new arrangement with you. Keep trying. Go up the the ladder, rung by rung, to the very top if you have to, until you find someone who does.

Once you've located that person, stick with him. If anyone else from the institution makes contact with you, don't get involved with her, simply refer her to the person with whom you're dealing. And stay in close touch with that person.

Glen, the actor, owed Chemical Bank $5,600 in credit card debt. His payment was $245 per month. When he tried to negotiate, successive representatives told him that nothing could be done; if he didn't pay as stipulated, the bank would take him to court. Glen kept trying. He finally got through to someone with authority, and spoke with him three separate times, holding firm to what was possible for him—he could pay no more than $35 a week. Each time the officer told him that this was unacceptable; the bank had no provision for weekly payments, nor would it take $140 per month. He warned that trouble was imminent.

Glen began to send $35 each week anyway. The officer protested and threatened, but Glen continued to send the money. Every Monday, Glen called the man at 9 A.M. to apprise him of what was going on in his life financially, told him what limo jobs he'd worked the previous week, what proofreading jobs, what auditions he'd been on. Eventually he developed a telephone relationship with the man that bordered on friendship. After several months, when Glen's situation had improved, he increased his payment to $50 a week.

Glen continued in this fashion for a year and a half, in

which he reduced his balance to $2,900. He was then able to raise his payments up not just to meet the minimum required each month, but in most months to more than that, and he liquidated the remaining balance without incident.

What was not possible, was possible.

Take the initiative. Get in touch with your creditors, explain your situation, express your commitment to repay them in full, and begin to negotiate.

A Simple Business Transaction

Keep firmly in mind that you are not in an inferior position when you negotiate with a creditor, regardless of any emotions you might have to the contrary.

What you are is one of two parties in a simple business transaction. You both want the same thing: You want the money to be repaid. All that's under discussion is the best way to do that. You know clearly what's possible for you and what isn't. Your job is to convey that information to your creditor.

Moratoriums and Restructuring

Some institutions will grant you a moratorium—a temporary suspension of payments—for three to six months if you need one and explain your problem clearly. Moratoriums are generally granted only on the principal; you continue to pay the interest or finance charges. For example, if your total monthly payment is $200—and that breaks down to $180 principal and $20 interest—you would pay $20 a month during the term of the moratorium.

Why would a creditor be willing to do this? Because it serves their self-interest. They don't want to see a default. They want their money back. For the same reason, they're often willing to restructure a loan—extend the time period over which it is to be paid off, which reduces the amount due each month.

Let's say, for example, that you have borrowed $3,500 from a bank at 15 percent interest, to be repaid in twelve monthly installments of $316. At your request, your bank restructures the loan, extending its term from one year to two years, now to be repaid in twenty-four installments instead of twelve. The restructuring will reduce your payment from $316 a month to $170 a month. You have just cut your total monthly expenses by $146, which can be a significant factor in balancing your Spending Plan to your income.

It's true that you'll pay more interest on the loan over twenty-four months than you would have over twelve. Interest for one year at 15 percent would have been $291. Interest over two years at 15 percent will be $572. That's $281 in additional interest. But what's important here is that you have lowered your monthly expenses by $146, your yearly expenses by $1,752. A cut like that can be crucial in the stabilizing phase of this program.

The point, remember, is to avoid taking on any new debt, one day at a time.

A Brief Word About Numbers

If the numbers in the last topic or anyplace else in the book confuse or intimidate you, don't worry about it. You don't have to master any complex formulas in order to work this program. All you really need to know in any given situation are the bottom-line figures—what it means in dollars you earn or dollars you have to pay; how much is going to principal, how much to interest.

If you're confused or uncertain at any point, just ask a friend who's good with numbers to go over the figures with you, or consult an accountant.

If you're asked to sign an agreement or document, you

need to understand what it means to you in real dollars and cents, so if you're unclear about that, consult with a qualified friend, an accountant, or a lawyer.

Consolidation Loans

To consolidate means to unite separate elements into a single unit. A *consolidation loan* is a single loan in an amount equal to the combined amount you owe to several different creditors. Say, for example, you owe a total of $20,000 to five different creditors. You apply to your bank for a consolidation loan in that amount. (The bank will usually require you to provide collateral such as a house or stock certificates as security.) If the loan is approved, the bank will pay off all your creditors, leaving you with only a single new creditor—the bank—to whom you owe $20,000.

At first glance, this might seem an excellent way to simplify things. But that glance can be deceptive. The monthly payment required by the bank frequently exceeds what most people with a debt problem can truly afford, which can lead right back to new debting in short order. It's generally best to avoid a consolidation loan, but if you do consider one, then do so carefully and with a clear picture of how much you can actually afford to repay each month.

Nonprofit Credit-Counseling Agencies

Nonprofit credit-counseling agencies have existed for half a century, but it was only in the 1990s that they exploded across the nation in great numbers, which continue to grow. These agencies claim, and in some cases advertise nationally, that they will act as your representative and negotiate with your creditors, getting better terms for you than you currently have. If you sign an agreement with one, it negotiates with your creditors on your behalf, and you send it a single check each month. The agency breaks your check down and disburses the appropriate amounts to your creditors. Sounds simple, appealing.

It is often neither.

Be wary of these agencies. Many are neither counseling organizations nor nonprofits in any but a technical sense. Many are predatory, and some just a notch above fraudulent.

The credit-counseling industry is a billion-dollar-a-year, largely unregulated business out of which an increasing number of horror stories are emerging. Some of these organizations are outright hustles. Others are run by executives with unsavory backgrounds, including violation of securities laws. Some top executives draw lavish salaries; some directors own businesses that provide services to the agencies for high fees; some officers have interests in outside financial organizations to which they refer clients. Fees can be steep and hidden, disguised under terms like "contributions."

Many people have been taken advantage of by such agencies, and some badly hurt, ending up owing more than they did before they began working with the agency and under greater pressure from creditors than before. This is definitely a case of caveat emptor: Let the buyer (or client) beware.

That said, it must also be said that legitimate and honest agencies do exist which have provided real help to debtors. Some of these are affiliated with an umbrella organization known as the National Foundation for Credit Counseling (NFCC). The NFCC accredits its members, who independently own 1,300 affiliated offices across the country. Many branches go under the name Consumer Credit Counseling Service. Some of these have good reputations. Some do not. You can locate the foundation online at http://www.debtadvice.org or be referred to an affiliated office near you by calling 800-388-2227.

There are disadvantages as well as advantages to working with a debt-counseling agency, even when it's a good one.

The longer your history with debt and the more serious your problem with it, the less likely any of these agencies will be of real help to you. They might even end up being hurtful.

The possible advantages are:

- Immediate help.
- An experienced advocate.
- You deal with one person, write one check.
- A reduction or even end to interest and a possible waiver of penalties.
- In most cases, you're out of debt in thirty-six months.

The disadvantages are:

- Little real counseling, nothing done to address and correct the problems that led to debt in the first place.
- Agencies won't work with everyone, some people are simply advised to declare bankruptcy.
- The standard repayment schedule is thirty-six months, which is often too brutal on the debtor, resulting in a deprived and unhappy life that may well lead to delinquency and ejection from the program.
- Agencies don't deal with personal creditors and some others, only with major commercial institutions and retailers.
- Deprives you of the opportunity to learn and accomplish, to reshape your relationship with money into something truly positive.
- Looks no better to a lender on your credit report than does having worked things out with your creditors yourself.
- May not give you enough information for you to know clearly what is happening and be sure your best interests are being served.

The most critical disadvantage is the failure to address why people get into trouble with debt in the first place and provide workable techniques through which to bring about change. As a result, many people get right back into trouble with debt again soon after they finish the agency's program.

If you do decide to work with one of these organizations, here are ten steps you can take to protect yourself:

1. Be alert, aware.
2. Use common sense.
3. Check for complaints against the agency with your Better Business Bureau and state attorney general's office before entering into an agreement with it.
4. Get a written statement that breaks your monthly payment down into principal and interest and names every creditor to whom payments will be made.
5. Get a statement of *all* fees you will be paying, regardless of what they might might be called.
6. Insist on a monthly statement—at the very least, quarterly—that shows exactly what your remaining balances are.
7. Monitor your account; read your statements and compare each to the previous one.
8. Be sure the agency is dealing with *all* your creditors. If it isn't, know exactly which ones are your responsibility.
9. Know how many months it will take you to liquidate your debt completely.
10. Take adult responsibility for yourself in the relationship.

For some debtors, working with such an agency might bring relief. But for a lasting solution, and a life with a real possibility of prosperity and abundance, anyone with a long history of incurring debt will need to undertake a comprehensive program of recovery from debting, whether he works with an agency or not.

The Contact Log

Keep a log of every contact you have with a creditor. Knowing precisely what you've discussed previously will minimize confusion and uncertainty in the future. This log can also be a powerful asset in the event a creditor brings legal action against you.

Keep the log in two parts. In the first, note all personal meetings and telephone conversations. In the second, keep copies of all correspondence—yours to them and theirs to you.

Use a large notebook to record the personal meetings and telephone calls. Under the creditor's name, enter the date of the meeting or call. Enter the name and title of the person with whom you spoke. Jot down a sentence or two to cover the substance of the discussion, and an adjective to characterize the attitude of whomever you dealt with. If you reached an agreement, be sure to enter its exact details. Then follow up with a letter confirming those details. Don't put the letter off. Send it the same afternoon or the following morning. This eliminates the chance of a misunderstanding on either side.

In the second part of the log, the correspondence file, make a separate file folder for each creditor. Make a carbon copy or photocopy of each letter you send, and place it in the appropriate file. Put every written communication you receive from that creditor in the same file. Keep the letters in chronological order so you have instant access to them.

The Reduction Record

The Reduction Record is a lot more than good and necessary record keeping—it shows you, month by month, your steady and unstoppable march toward total freedom from debt. It is a source of confidence, self-esteem, and pleasure. To start one:

1. Get a loose-leaf binder.
2. Leave the first page blank.
3. On a separate page for each debt write the date, the creditor's name, and the current amount of the debt.
4. Each month, immediately after you send out your repayment checks, enter on the appropriate page the amount of principal you repaid, *regardless of how small that amount might be*, and the date you paid it.
5. Subtract that payment from the current balance.
6. Enter the new balance.

Here is what one of my own pages looked like, back in the beginning years:

BOB $500   SEPTEMBER 14, 1984

DATE	BALANCE
	$500.00
10-01-84	−5.00
	495.00
11-01-84	−5.00
	490.00
12-03-84	−5.16
	484.84
01-02-85	−5.64
	479.20
02-03-85	−6.12
	473.08
03-04-85	−6.12
	466.96
04-01-85	−6.80
	460.16

Payments continued in this fashion through 1985 and into 1986, rising each month as my income increased and as I adusted my Repayment Plan accordingly. The last three appear as follows:

Date	Balance
	127.30
07-01-86	−35.70
	91.60
08-01-86	−41.60
	50.00
09-01-86	−50.00
	PAID

The Liquidation Record

If the Reduction Record is a pleasure, the Liquidation Record is a joy.

On the top of the first page in your binder—the one you left blank—write "Liquidation Record." As you make the final payment on any debt, no matter how small or insignificant that debt seemed, write it down. Enter the name of your former creditor, the original amount of the debt, and the date you paid it off. For example:

Creditor	Amount	Liquidated
American Express	$1,066	July 10, 2000
Citibank—Visa	$2,405	June 1, 2001
Frances	$750	September 1, 2002

Look at this page each month, just before you enter your most recent payments in the Reduction Record. It is absolute proof that you are on your way to total freedom from debt.

18

HERE LIE MONSTERS
(IF YOU THINK SO)

On ancient maps, certain vaguely known regions of water or land were sometimes marked, "Here Lie Monsters," and embellished with depictions of sea serpents and other dreadful creatures. Today, certain areas of many people's minds are similarly marked, and populated with such fearsome entities as the Collection Agency, the Court Judgment, and the Bad Credit Rating. Unlike the fanciful beasts of old, some of these actually exist. But they are monsters only if you think they are.

Reflect for a moment upon everything you've learned up to now, the clarity you have, the command you've taken of your money and life, the strength you've gained. You're not the same person you were when you began this book.

There are no monsters, only problems, which can be dealt with and resolved.

The Customer Account Department

The section within an institution that deals with your account—your debt—is the customer account department. If you cannot pay the monthly figure required, then you'll have to work out an adjustment. Your first step is to make contact with the customer account department.

If the debt is a formal bank loan, then either a moratorium or restructuring will be necessary. Make an appointment to discuss it with the officer you originally saw when you took out the loan. If the debt is a form of consumer credit such as a charge account at a department store, then get in touch with the customer account department. Present your problem as you would to any other creditor, according to the guidelines already outlined.

Many of these creditors will be willing to work out an agreement with you; it's generally simpler and more profitable for them to do so than to turn your account over to a collection agency or go to court against you. Some will refuse. But even in these cases, it is still sometimes possible to pay them according to *your* Repayment Plan rather than theirs.

Many people have done so on a unilateral basis. Nicole owed Lord & Taylor $975. Her monthly payment was $210. She acknowledged the debt, stated her commitment to repay it, explained her situation, and gave them all the pertinent figures, which clearly indicated that she could pay no more than $65 a month. They refused to accept this. She went ahead anyway, mailing in her payments according to her own plan, just as Glen did with Chemical Bank. Despite the store's repeated protests, her payments were accepted and no action was taken against her.

If you choose this route, keep the following points in mind:

1. Regardless of the amount of principal you repay, be sure to pay the *complete* finance charge (interest) each month. If you don't, that will be added to your existing balance, which is in effect a new debt. It may also provoke the creditor into action against you.
2. Be reliable. Send the amount you told the creditor you would send, and send it on time.

3. Stay in touch with the creditor on a regular basis. Keep them informed of your situation and aware of your commitment to repay them in full.

A creditor is under no obligation to accept such a unilateral agreement, but many will. What happens when they won't is discussed in the following topic and again later in this chapter.

Collection Agencies

A collection agency is an organization whose sole function is to collect money from people who have failed to pay a bill or who have defaulted on a debt. Any creditor may turn a defaulted account over to a collection agency.

Most creditors, however, would prefer to resolve the situation with you themselves rather than resort to a collection agency. Why? Because if they use a collection agency, they lose money.

The moment an account goes into collection it comes under the protection of state usury laws, which put a cap on the rate of interest that can be charged. The cap varies from state to state, but is usually 9 or 10 percent, which is substantially less than the creditor has been getting from you—in most cases 19 to 21 percent. This is significant, since most retailers today are not simply retailers; they're in the lending business as well. A large part of their profits derive from finance charges on their time-payment accounts.

Further, a collection agency, as its fee, keeps anywhere from 18 to 50 percent of everything it collects. So not only does the creditor take a cut in interest, but it loses 18¢ to 50¢ on the dollar as well.

But let's assume that despite your best efforts a creditor remains intractable and puts your account into collection. Collection agencies can be tough, which isn't surprising.

They get the hard cases—people who are in deep financial trouble, or who've ignored their creditors or are trying to beat them, or who've run out on bills.

Deal with a collection agency as you would with any other creditor, following the guidelines. But don't expect to be welcomed with open arms. They've heard every excuse, promise, and con job in the book. They have no reason to think you're any different from all the others they've dealt with.

But you are. And it's your job to impress that upon them. Be persistent.

Jean is a young woman who works as a word processor. Two of her debts—$1,600 to Bloomingdale's and $750 to Lord & Taylor—were in the hands of a collection agency. Her Repayment Plan called for $40 a month to Bloomingdale's and $28 to Lord & Taylor. The agency demanded $125 a month for Bloomingdale's and an immediate payment of $375 for Lord & Taylor, the balance within two months. They took her to court. A judge's assistant sent them home, instructing them to keep talking and to try to reach agreement. If they could not, they were to appear in court again the following month. That month, the agency refused to negotiate with Jean at all. However, at the next court appearance the agency's lawyer, to Jean's surprise, told the court they would take $80 a month for Bloomingdale's and $50 for Lord & Taylor. Jean could still not pay those amounts without incurring new debt. The court instructed them to try once again, and sent them away a second time. This time Jean wrote directly to the head of the agency, set forth her situation in precise detail, enclosed two checks—one for $40 and the other for $28, the amounts she had originally offered—and asked that her schedule be accepted. It was, and no further legal action was taken.

Keep in mind that you are beyond the ken of a collection agency's previous experience—you're taking the initiative, you're armed with the facts and figures, you know precisely what you're doing; you're dealing with them honestly and you're trying to find a way to pay back the money you owe. That makes you a rare person in their experience.

You might be able to make an agreement, you might not. If you can't, you might consider instituting a unilateral Repayment Plan anyway, sending a check each month in the amount you said you would. This has sometimes proved successful and no legal action has been taken.

Collection agencies are governed by clear laws. Most abide by them, but some do not. A collection agent is forbidden from harassing, threatening, or abusing you. He can not imply that he is an attorney, a private detective, or that he represents a credit bureau. He can't telephone you before 8 A.M. or after 9 P.M. without your permission. She can not inform your employer or anyone else that you owe money. She can't make contact with other people about you unless it is to inquire about your whereabouts. She must cease contact with you if you tell her to do so in writing, and may only get in touch again if it is to inform you that she or your creditor is undertaking legal action against you.

If you have the misfortune to run into an unscrupulous agency, report it at once to your state attorney general's office and your local consumer affairs bureau, and file a complaint with the Federal Trade Commission. You can do the latter online at http://www.ftc.gov or by mail at:

Federal Trade Commission
Consumer Protection Bureau
Credit Practices Division
Washington, DC 20580
Telephone: 202-326-2222

The FTC will not come bounding to your defense but it will log your complaint, and if a pattern of abuse is found around a particular agency it will take action against the agency. You may be able to get direct help through your local consumer advocate, ombudsman, or media consumer reporter.

The IRS

You *will* pay any back taxes you owe, and the penalties and interest. But there are options. The Internal Revenue Service is not irrational or without understanding. Approach them as you would any other creditor—honestly, and with complete documentation of your situation. They are stern and determined, but in most cases a livable payment schedule can be negotiated.

The same is true of most state and local agencies too.

It's Not a Court of Inquisition

If you work this program, the odds are you won't end up in court. But sometimes, despite your best efforts, it happens. It's not possible to cover every situation—different states have different laws, and credit contracts vary—but we *can* set up a general model to follow if you do have to appear in court.

Let's assume that your efforts to negotiate an agreement compatible with your commitment not to incur new debt have failed and that a creditor goes to court against you. The creditor is required to serve you with a summons. You are required to appear at the office of the court clerk to answer the summons. If you don't, the court will hand down a judgment against you. This judgment opens the way to a salary garnishment, which is a court order instructing your employer to withhold a portion of your salary until the debt has been paid. The portion is limited to 25 percent of your after-tax income by federal law and to less than that by some state laws, which take precedence.

Sometimes a debtor is shocked to receive notice that a judgment has been entered against him—when he never even received a summons and didn't know that a creditor had filed against him. This is usually the result of what's known as "sewer service": A process server warrants to the creditor that he did indeed serve the summons, but what really happened was that he simply dumped the summons, along with many others, down a sewer. In some parts of the country, this is considered a cheaper way to handle things than to serve the summons. It is, of course, an illegal practice.

If this happens to you, register a complaint with your state attorney general's office immediately and go at once to the court where the judgment was entered. Tell the court clerk that you want to make a motion to set aside the judgment because you were never served. The judgment will be set aside. Eventually, you will be properly served.

When you are served, you have twenty to thirty days from the date you *receive* the summons to make your answer, regardless of the date the summons was issued. To answer, go to the office of the court clerk. Tell the clerk that you want a hearing. Do *not* state or sign anything that represents agreement with your creditor's claim. Insist upon a hearing.

You *want* your day in court.

Many people are intimidated by the idea of court, but without cause. It is *not* a Court of Inquisition. It is *not* there to punish or deprive you. It is *not* a place where your creditor's demands will receive a rubber stamp of approval. The purpose of the court is to give a fair hearing to both parties—to *you* as well as your creditor. And that, if you have been working this program, is to your great advantage.

Most debtors never ask for a court hearing. Of those who do, the majority are in a fog about their money and debts and either angry, belligerent, or paralyzed by fear. You are none of these now.

When you go to court, do so in the following way:

1. Prepare well in advance.
2. Document your income and assets.
3. Document your monthly expenses, using your Spending Plan to demonstrate where your money goes.
4. Document your total debt structure.
5. Bring your Repayment Plan.
6. Bring your Contact Log, which contains a record of all the meetings, telephone calls, and correspondence you've had with your creditor.
7. Acknowledge the debt.
8. State your commitment to repay in full.
9. Explain that you are in a financial recovery process and committed to not incurring new debt.
10. Disclose your membership in a support group, if you are comfortable doing that.

When you approach a hearing in this manner, here is what the court sees: a person who fully acknowledges her debt and states her commitment to repay it; who presents concrete evidence that not only did she not attempt to evade her creditor but that she herself initiated the contact; and who tried repeatedly in good faith to negotiate a reasonable repayment schedule. Further, she brings with her a detailed statement of her income and expenses, a statement of her total indebtedness, and a figure that accurately represents what she is able to repay each month. The court sees a person committed to her own recovery and determined not to incur new debt.

This sets you miles apart from the average debtor in the court's experience. Your creditor knows this and will frequently capitulate at the last moment, before the case goes before the judge.

Stan, a computer programmer, owed $5,100 in credit card debt to Chase Bank. He had tried to negotiate for several months. His Repayment Plan allowed him to offer them $137 a month. They insisted on $228. He began sending the

$137 anyway. They cashed his checks but refused to accept his plan. Eventually they did file against him. Stan appeared in court, answered "Here" when the roll was called, then sat waiting calmly, his attaché case with all his documentation beside him. The clerk informed him and the bank's lawyer that his case would be called next.

The lawyer looked at Stan several moments, then said, "All right, we'll take the $137."

They signed a written agreement (*always* get such an agreement in writing), informed the clerk that a settlement had been reached, and the case was never heard.

If the case does go to the bench, what usually happens—if you have carefully followed the guidelines above—is that the judge rules the creditor must accept your repayment schedule. Why does this happen? Because the court is neither arbitrary nor irrational. It recognizes your commitment to repay, and you have placed substantial evidence before it to back up your claim that you can not reasonably pay more than you have already offered to pay.

Sy, a therapist, owed Citibank $2,600 in credit card debt, with a payment of $98 due each month. This $2,600 represented 7 percent of Sy's total debt. He could repay a total of $405 each month toward all his debts. Seven percent of that, Citibank's share, was $28, and that was all he could offer them. They took him to court. The judge examined Sy's supporting evidence, his correspondence file, and Contact Log, and ruled that the bank had to accept the $28 per month. He rebuked the bank's attorney. "What are you wasting the court's time for?" he said. "This man made plain to you what was possible and offered you the best payback he could."

Jean, the word processor we previously cited, was also in credit card debt to Citibank for $4,000, on which $167 a month was due. At that time she had just begun this program. She requested a three-month moratorium in which to determine what was possible for her. They refused and took her to court. She brought her documentation and explained her situation. The judge granted her the moratorium. At the end of the moratorium, Jean presented to the bank a profile of her indebtedness along with a copy of her Spending and Repayment plans. She could pay them $81 a month. They took her to court again, and the judge ruled that they had to accept her Repayment Plan.

Showing up, undergoing this sort of thing, and sticking to your purpose is not easy. It requires effort, strength, and determination. But it is very much to your benefit to do so and can be a large step forward in your recovery and in the growth of your self-confidence and self-esteem.

You can neither expect nor hope for a positive outcome, though, if you have not been honest with yourself or your creditor. It is irrational, for example, to expect the court to support your contention that you can pay only $100 a month against a $10,000 debt if you're driving a $30,000 automobile, living in a $3,500 a month penthouse, and spending $800 a month on entertainment. The court will not do this—nor should it. Honesty and fairness are crucial to achieving a successful day in court.

There are no guarantees here. Still, I don't know a single case in which someone working this program was ordered to meet a payment schedule beyond his or her means, or subjected to a salary garnishment.

The Credit Rating, Or: Whose Graven Image Is This?

To most people, a Bad Credit Rating is a terrifying prospect. The Credit Rating has become nearly an object of worship in contemporary society. Its power is unspeakable. It fills us with awe. So long as we have a Good Credit Rating, we are safe, and all is well with the world. Should we be stricken by a Bad Credit Rating, we will be abandoned and forlorn, plunged into chaos, and condemned to wander help-less through a hostile wilderness.

Actually, there is no such thing as a personal credit rating. What there are, are credit reports—printouts of computer-ized records maintained by commercial credit bureaus. These records are kept on every individual who has ever used commercial credit. They contain information collected by the bureaus from stores with whom you have dealt, from banks and other lending institutions, and from public records and other sources. Any time you apply for commer-cial credit in any form, including mortgages, credit cards, and store accounts, the prospective lender will obtain a credit report on you from one of these bureaus. So will land-lords, insurance agents, and in many cases employers. This report will contain a detailed history of your borrowing and repayment patterns, including cancellations of accounts, de-faults, actions by collection agencies, and court proceedings against you. It will even note whether you tend to pay your monthly bills within thirty, sixty, or ninety days. The credit bureau itself makes no judgment as to whether you are a good credit risk, although its report generally does include a score. This score is based on a formula that considers other factors as well as your payment history, among them are the number of credit cards you have and how long you have lived at your current address. The most common scoring sys-tem is known as FICO (Fair, Isaac and Company, Inc.). The bureau simply provides a report. The lender is the one who makes the decision, based on the information within the re-port.

But whether we call it a rating, a record, or a report, the prospect of a bad one scares the hell out of most people—particularly those with debt trouble—and they'll agree to practically any demand from a creditor to avoid one.

We are threatened: "Pay up, or this'll go on your record."

It's true. If a store cancels your account, if a bank cancels your credit card, if the court hands down a judgment against you, if you default on a student loan, if the IRS places a lien against you, it all goes on to your record; the credit bureaus enter the information into their computers and henceforth it appears, like a great scarlet letter, on all reports issued on you.

You have a Bad Credit Record.

Cry woe and lamentation! Oh God! Nothing could be worse, right?

Wrong. Many things could. In fact, the Bad Credit Record isn't very high up on the list of Terrible Things.

After reading an announcement of his own demise in a newspaper, Mark Twain wrote to the editor: "The reports of my death have been greatly exaggerated."

So, for people with a debt problem, has the significance of the Credit Record. What can you do with a good one? Basically, use it to borrow money, to go into debt. Since you don't do that anymore, a credit record—good, bad, or indifferent—really doesn't mean that much to you, does it?

I don't suggest that you go out and stomp all over yours just for the hell of it. But I do suggest that if you are in recovery from debting, and a creditor is using it as a club with which to beat you, that you reconsider its importance. It's largely a paper club. It can't hurt you mortally.

If you do end up with a bad credit record—which is by no means certain, regardless of what your creditors tell you (remember, you have options now, from renegotiation to your day in court)—about the worst that will happen is that you'll be unable to get any new credit cards or charge accounts. Which is irrelevant, since you don't debt anymore.

"But I won't be able to buy a car if I don't have a good credit record."

That's not true. You might have to do a little shopping among dealers or banks, but even people who have declared bankruptcy can get a car loan without much trouble, remember? A car is first-rate collateral.

"Well, maybe a car, but I know I can't get a mortgage to buy a house or a co-op if I have a bad credit record."

You think you know that.

Howard is a market researcher with a bad credit record. His report shows a slew of canceled credit cards and department store accounts, a couple of court judgments and an old lien for unpaid taxes; all the legacy of his debting days, which ended seven years ago. He's been working the principles of this program ever since. Three years ago, he liquidated the last of his original $49,000 debt. A year prior to that, his building went co-op. Despite his bad credit record and the fact that he was still carrying $7,000 worth of debt, Howard bought his apartment for $178,000. He did it with a $145,000 mortgage. A year later, he took out a second mortgage for $20,000 to finance a business expansion. Six months ago, he relocated to another city, sold his apartment for $348,000, and bought a house in the new city for $567,000, financing it with a $445,000 mortgage.

What Howard did was to get from his accountant the name of a lawyer who dealt with the local financial institutions. Howard explained to the lawyer his history and his recovery in this program, reviewed the state of his current finances with him, then hired him to represent him in seeking a mortgage. The lawyer found a bank willing to grant Howard a mortgage—under standard terms, no extra points or premiums—on the first try.

Others have had to go to two or three banks. Sometimes four or five. The point is, if you really want that house, and can afford it, you can get a mortgage. Some people have arranged it themselves; others, like Howard, have hired a representative to do it for them. If you have the money and if the house is worth the asking price, you'll be able to find a bank that will give you a mortgage.

Credit records change, and can be changed. After a period of seven years, a blot such as a canceled account or a judgment is automatically deleted from your record. It's as if it

never existed. You can also file a statement of explanation—
if you think there are mitigating circumstances—with any
credit bureau that carries your record. They are required by
law to include it in their reports on you. And if you have liquidated debts that still appear on your record as unpaid, the
credit bureau must correct your record if you request them
to and submit proof that the debt has been paid.

Now, as with all graven images, beneath the image there
actually is some reality: Life *is* more difficult with a bad
credit record. It is easier to buy a home, get a job, rent an
apartment, finance a car, and take out an insurance policy
with a good one than with a bad one. With a good record,
you may also be able to avoid cash deposits when you establish accounts with telephone, electric, gas, heating oil, water,
and cable TV companies. Potential employers often use a
credit check to get a sense of an applicant's character, honesty, and integrity. Landlords do the same. So indeed things
are easier with a good credit record than with a bad one.

However, things aren't impossible with a bad credit
record, just more difficult. At least for people in recovery. For
people who aren't, a bad credit record can be a serious challenge and liability. By committing to your recovery and
practicing this program, you can largely neutralize the impact of a bad credit record. After a year or more of not incurring any new debt, and having negotiated with your
creditors, established a repayment plan and begun repayments, and perhaps even increased your income, you'll be
able to offer a reasonable preemptive statement to a prospective employer, landlord, or credit grantor about what it's
going to find when it runs a credit check on you. You'll be
able to demonstrate that you have turned things around and
have been repaying your creditors steadily and reliably for
some time now.

The key here is to be proactive: Tell whoever is about to
request your credit report what she will find in it. Tell her
before she finds it. This prevents her from being unpleas-

antly surprised. It casts you as forthright. It gives you an opportunity to explain and to point out your history of steady repayment and even liquidation of these old debts over the past year or more, which mitigates and may even eliminate the negative impact of your record. This is what I did myself in the late 1980s when I left New York for a while and went down South to help create and edit a magazine and needed to buy a car there. The financing went through easily, and at no extra points.

With most credit grantors or interested parties, you can probably handle this preemptive disclosure and explanation yourself. If you're buying a house, co-op, or condominium, it's best to consult with an attorney and probably to hire him to be your advocate, as Howard did. The stakes are high and some of the protocols complicated.

If you have a poor credit record, you will most likely want to rebuild it in time, which we'll discuss in the next chapter. For now, just know that regardless of what your creditors might tell you, a good credit record is not the sine qua non of success. Nor does a bad one sentence you to impoverishment or restrict you in any truly meaningful way.

Like the reports of Mark Twain's death, a credit record's significance, for people who don't debt, has been greatly exaggerated.

19

SUPPORTS

The chapter contains material that will help you in working other parts of the Back to the Black program.

HALT

HALT is an acronym: Don't get too Hungry, too Angry, too Lonely, or too Tired. It's corny, but it works.

When you're hungry, your blood sugar drops. This interferes with your concentration, diminishes your intellectual capacities, and causes your emotions to take a turn for the worse. Things look bleaker, more difficult. You're not in the best shape to plan or make decisions. Try to eat on a regular schedule. If you feel your mood begin to slip, think back to your last meal. Maybe all you need is something to eat—cheese, fruit, a sandwich. Avoid heavy sweets, which can toss your blood sugar up and down.

Anger—justified or unjustified—is destructive. You hurt yourself when you act or speak out of anger. You don't think clearly, you burn bridges and cut off your nose to spite your face. You provoke anger in others. Even if you're alone, it simply eats at you, dominating your thoughts and emotions, and accomplishes nothing. Distance and distract yourself from it.

Everyone is lonely at times. It's not pleasant, but it's not lethal either. People get on with their lives in spite of it. But excessive loneliness—more accurately, isolation—is something else. Loneliness and isolation feed upon each other. The lonelier you get, the more you isolate; and the more you isolate, the lonelier you get. This isolation, this increasing disconnection from life, is a fertile breeding ground for distorted attitudes and perceptions. The more you remain alone with your own thoughts and moods, the darker, more skewed, and more distorted they become and the more hopeless things begin to look. As with anger, the best thing to do is distance and distract yourself from it. Arrange to meet friends, get in touch with members of your support group; at the very least, go to a movie, read a book, get active around the house, go to a gym. Force yourself to take action—it's action that will lead to a change of mood, not the other way around.

When you're tired, go to bed. Don't push yourself. You can't think clearly then. Your capacity to reason is impaired. You become more vulnerable to loneliness and mood swings.

P.S., Your Furnace Is Dead

What do you do when your car breaks down in the morning, your oldest child calls later to tell you the dog ate the sofa, you lose your biggest account in the afternoon, and when you get home in the evening you find a note from the plumber saying he replaced the living room baseboard, and P.S., your furnace is dead? You express deep gratitude for your contingency fund, that's what.

A contingency is something unforeseen that occurs by chance. Contingencies happen to everyone. Some of them cost money.

A contingency fund is a set amount of money you keep apart from your other funds. It should be liquid—available to you immediately. A special savings or money-market account is a good place for it. Don't mix it in with your other money. This fund covers you in times of emergency or unexpected expenses. It's your own insurance policy.

Remember the margin we spoke about in Chapter 12? We suggested that after you'd stabilized—matched income to expenses—and begun to bring in more than is called for by your initial Spending Plan, that you spread half of that surplus through the categories you'd most like to increase and put the other half into savings. These savings are your contingency fund.

Keep building the fund until it's complete, until you've reached whatever amount you have decided is enough. How much is enough? That varies from person to person. For most, it's an amount equal to three months' total expenses, enough to cover every expense on your Spending Plan even if everything were to go completely to hell and you couldn't bring in a dollar for the entire period. Self-employed people generally need more than this, enough for six to twelve months.

The contingency fund is not a bonus or gravy fund from which to draw at will or whim when you simply get an urge to buy a new pair of shoes, take a weekend in the mountains, or go out to an expensive dinner. Using it that way would deplete it in fairly short order despite your best intentions and leave you as vulnerable as you were before. This fund is a safety net. If you miss your handhold, if something goes wrong, you don't have to worry—you've got your contingency fund to catch you. It should remain intact at all times. Use it only in the event of a major, necessary, and unforeseen expense, such as unexpected dental work or automobile repair, and replace the amount you withdraw from it as quickly as possible. You should maintain the fund at the level you originally set for it, unless you decide that figure is too low and you want to raise it.

Once you've built your contingency fund, you can apply the money you were formerly depositing into it to whatever other purpose you desire.

"Keel the Bool"

A poor Spanish peasant, goes an old story, returns to his tiny hut where there is not even firewood. His wife and son are huddled under a blanket eating the last crumbs of bread. He tells them that men from the city wish to buy their bull to fight in the bullring.

"Oh no!" cries the boy. "Not the bool. Not my favorite thing in the whole world, not my friend. Not the bool I raised from a little calf!"

"But, my son," says the peasant, "we have no money left and nothing to eat. They will pay us $30,000 for him. We can move to a house. You will have shoes, a bicycle. You will be able to go to movies, to go to school, to have all the things you never had before."

"$30,000?" the boy asks.

"Yes, my son."

"Shoes? A bicycle? School?"

"Everything, my son."

The boy reflects a moment, then says brightly, "Keel the bool."

This is extreme, perhaps, but it makes the point. When you're in trouble, when you *need* money, when it's a question of holding the line or falling into new debt again, do you look upon a particular object as a prized possession—something over which you'd rather have your fingernails torn out than to part with—or as a valuable asset that can be converted to cash in order to serve your needs?

It's a question of perception that generally arises in the early stages of recovery, when things may be tight and any given day a challenge.

A year into this program, I had to make that kind of decision. I owned a 1961 Ford convertible, a popular historical automobile I'd originally bought for pleasure and as an investment, to turn over when my youngest son went to college. I enjoyed that car, and it had taken me nearly two years to persuade its owner to sell it to me. But when I needed the money to follow this program, in order not to debt, I sold the car. And at another point an antique mirror, and later a hundred-year-old carved wooden statue of a Hindu god.

I liked all three of those. There was discomfort involved in selling them. Then, and in other situations, I would have preferred alternative scenarios, but I have never regretted any action I've ever taken to maintain my solvency, to avoid incurring new debt. Nor do I know anyone else who has either.

If things seem impossible, take another look around at what you own. Sometimes it's simply a matter of perception— is that a prized possession or is it a valuable asset?

Rainy Days

Saving money for a rainy day is a bad idea.

Surprised? Many of us were taught early on that we'd better sock money away toward catastrophe or for our old age. But that kind of "saving" has destructive consequences. It builds a poverty mentality. It tells you that there's not much now, and that there will be even less in the future. Or that while things may look fine today, you'd better be careful, you never know when disaster will strike. Don't be a grasshopper singing in the sunlight, we're told, be a busy ant storing up toward the lean times ahead.

People who put all their money away toward catastrophe live in increasing fear of catastrophe. That very fear is likely to *create* such an event—just as a driver who's nervous and apprehensive about an accident is more likely to cause one than is a confident and relaxed driver who's enjoying his trip. Or they may come to resent what they feel is an obligation to save, and swing to the opposite pole, begin to spend up to or past the limit of their income. Or they may subconsciously trigger an emergency in order to release back into their lives what they've already put away. Whatever the outcome, hoarding leads to a sense of restriction, privation, and the idea that there is never enough.

Maria is a film editor who had been brutalized by a twelve-year history of debting and underearning. Her primary emotions, by the end, were rage and terror. She was only three months into this program when her father died, leaving her an inheritance of $175,000. She put it all in a savings account and refused to touch a penny of it. Several months later, she lost her job. After two months of being out of work, she was nearly incapacitated by fear.

"I can't pay the rent!" she cried. "I don't have any money for food!"

She'd always been secretive about money and had told only one close friend about the inheritance. That woman pointed out to her that she *did* have money, that she *could* pay the rent and buy food.

Maria grew hysterical. "I can't touch that! I need it. You know how old people live when they don't have any money. I'd kill myself before I'd live like that. I can't touch that money!"

Her terror of a possibility some thirty years in the future had made that possibility into reality right now: She was penniless, hopeless, and helpless.

With her friend's help, Maria began to speak openly at her support group. Gradually she began to calm, and finally she recognized she was alive and had needs *today*. She was still frightened and resistant, but she drew upon the money. That enabled her to break her emotional paralysis and begin to take action. She found a new job several weeks later. In a few months, she became willing to draw up and implement a Repayment Plan. (She could have liquidated all of her $15,000 debt at once, but both she and her support group felt it would be better for her to pay it off in a steady, planned fashion over a twenty-four-month period; as a discipline, to help her learn a new style of life and a new way of handling her financial affairs.)

Today, three years later, Maria is debt-free. She's earning 30 percent more than she did on her previous job and lives better and more happily than she ever did before. And she has built her original $175,000 inheritance into $190,000— not hoarded in a savings account against a threatening future, but invested in income-producing assets that are a part of her ongoing prosperity.

I'm not suggesting that you say to hell with tomorrow and live strictly for today, but I am suggesting that you look upon your surplus income in a new light. Your contingency fund will cover most of the curveballs life is going to throw at you. Continuing simply to store up is overkill. In general, the best thing to do with your money as it increases is to spread a portion of the surplus through your Spending Plan, steadily improving the quality of your life and your daily sense of well-being, and to invest the rest rather than simply to "save" it.

Investing has nothing to do with get-rich-quick schemes or making a killing in the market. It's putting money to work for you, rather than you working for it—safely, and in ways that will bring you a return that exceeds the rate of inflation. Consult with a qualified financial planner who can explain the possibilities to you. He or she will tailor a plan to your own needs and goals.

Savings are not something to store up for emergencies or for parsimonious use in your old age. They are assets, to be seen as yet another source of increase, benefit, and pleasure, as a part of your prosperity.

An Additional Note on Secured Loans

We discussed secured loans in detail in Part I. There is one more point to make about them, which we deferred until now so that we could make it in the context of a deeper understanding of the Back to the Black program than was possible in the early chapters.

Putting up collateral to secure a loan you need in order to meet expenses without debting can make a crucial difference when you're still in the process of stabilizing, and sometimes later on too, particularly among self-employed people or others whose income may be erratic. At any point, it is vital to do whatever needs to be done to avoid new debt.

However, it's best not to use a secured loan simply to cover your basic needs, if that is at all possible. It's better to cut expenses, generate additional income, or sell something outright. Taking a secured loan in order to meet ordinary needs still leaves a disparity between income and expenses, a situation that cannot continue indefinitely. Sooner or later, that will lead to debt. Further, if you can't repay the loan you'll have to forfeit your collateral, which is depressing and which will tempt you to think that somehow you've failed.

The *primary* purpose of a secured loan is to help you in making a major purchase, such as a house. Here, the criterion is: Can you afford it, do the monthly payments fit easily into your Spending Plan? If the answer is yes, there's no reason not to go ahead. If the answer is no, it would be self-destructive even to think about it. In the main, secured loans should not be used for general living expenses.

Briefly, on Rebuilding a Credit Record

As we pointed out earlier, the primary benefit of having a good credit record is that you can borrow money—that is, go into debt. Which, for a debtor, will stop recovery cold and usually signals the start of the same sad story all over again. But we also granted that life *is* easier with a good credit record, and that there are advantages to having one. So it will probably make sense, once you're solidly grounded in your recovery, to rebuild your credit record.

Be careful in this. Extremely careful. Your primary goal—always—is to remain solvent. You can't toy with debting. With that in mind, here are four basic steps you can take to reestablish a good record. You'll need a year or two to rebuild your record to the point where a prospective employer or lender will begin to look upon it favorably. Remember, carefulness and caution are important here.

One: Begin rebuilding on a foundation of genuine recovery. Anything less, and you're likely to crash and burn and end up with nothing but a bigger problem than you had before. Belonging to a support group is helpful. At the least, enlist the help of a trusted friend who is financially healthy. He or she will be your confidant and ally, to whom you can explain what you're doing, with whom you can check in regularly and report your actions and progress, and who, should such prove desirable, can help you as discussed below. Checking in regularly with this person can help you avoid the real and dangerous pitfalls that exist here for a debtor.

Two: Be timely with all your payments. Don't be late with or miss even a single one. Late or missed payments can destroy a credit record. Fortunately, this step should be easy for you since—glad to say—you don't debt anymore.

Three: Obtain a secured credit card. This involves placing an amount of money on deposit with the issuing bank, usually $300 to $2,500. The bank then gives you a Visa or MasterCard which looks just like an unsecured card and which can be used in the same way—except that you can charge on it only up to the amount you have on deposit (the security). When the bill arrives, pay it in full (restoring the balance of your security and thus the amount you can charge again) or pay the minimum required or a bit more (adding that amount back to your deposit, minus whatever part is for interest). If you miss a payment, the payment will be deducted from your deposit. You won't have incurred unsecured debt in that case, since the payment was covered by what you had on deposit, but you will have defeated the purpose of having gotten a secured card in the first place. You will only have worsened your record with yet another, and very recent, black mark. A late payment is as damaging as a missed payment.

Be aware that some issuers offer unsecured credit on top of the secured amount—$1,500 worth of charging privileges, say, on a $1,000 deposit—and thus pose a danger to your solvency. The only thing you can do with that unsecured credit is debt. So use an issuer that limits the amount you can charge to the amount of your deposit.

Be aware, too, that there are gougers in this industry. Some issuers charge application fees, setup fees, and administration fees for a secured card. Avoid these. Also, shop around for the best interest rate on balances. Currently these rates are running from 9 percent all the way up to 21 percent. A good online source for comparison at this writing is http://www.bankrate.com.

Once you have a secured card, use it. Make a small purchase or two every month or every other month and pay the bill, or at least the minimum required, as soon as it arrives. Simply having a card won't help your credit record. It is the steady paying each month according to terms that employers and lenders look for.

After a year of timely payments, request that the issuer convert your card into a standard, unsecured version. This is a potentially dangerous move for a debtor, which is why rebuilding should only be undertaken on a solid foundation of recovery, and a circumstance in which your trusted confidant and ally can be particularly helpful. Use your new unsecured card just as you did your secured card, making occasional small purchases. When the bill arrives, pay it in full or—having self-secured it—pay the minimum required or more and liquidate what's left after a couple of months. How can you secure an unsecured card yourself? By depositing into a special savings account or an envelope at home enough money to cover the total you've charged or intend to, or even better, by giving it over for safekeeping to your confidant and ally. Then when the bill comes in you can draw out from the account or envelope or get back from your friend however much you intend to pay that month. Either way will work, so far as not-debting goes. But don't even *think* about getting an unsecured card and securing it yourself unless you are certain of your solvency. Otherwise all you'll be doing is sharpening a stake on which you're eventually likely to impale yourself.

Four: Create a second source of credit. Paying one lender according to terms is helpful, paying two is better. This second source can be another card or a personal loan from your bank or credit union. It's easier to get a personal loan if you can offer collateral: equities, a certificate of deposit, title to a car, other property. Securing the loan will also bring a lower interest rate. If you can't offer security, you might still be able to get a loan, especially if you have a good relationship with your bank. Ask for the smallest amount offered, usually $500. Secured or unsecured, the bank will want to see a good credit report on you and will want your account to be free of bounced checks. Which, of course, is the Catch-22 you're facing. Be candid with your loan officer. Explain to her what you're doing. When she fully understands, and since you can demonstrate a clean record for the past year or more, you have a reasonable chance of getting the loan.

If you do get the loan, self-secure it in the manner already described. It will be an installment loan, that is, will have a specified life, generally from six to thirty-six months, over which you are to repay it in equal monthly installments. The most effective way to manage an installment loan in this circumstance is to make two or three monthly payments, then pay off the balance in full. (There is no penalty for paying an installment loan off early; and you'll also save interest.) This will get the desired information entered into your record. If you can't get a personal loan, open a department store account or obtain a second credit card.

Finally, in closing this topic, avoid commercial services that claim they will rebuild your credit for a price. They won't, or can't. Most are little more than hustles, and even the best of them (which isn't saying much) can't do anything more for you than you can do for yourself.

I'll Drink to That

Maybe, but it's usually better not to.

Chemical mood-changers—from alcohol, marijuana, and cocaine to prescription tranquilizers and energizers—don't mix any better with debt than they do with driving. The relief or comfort they might seem to provide is illusory. Even mild use of them over an extended period can subtly distort your attitudes, perceptions, and judgments. They interfere with your emotions and thought processes, and the effects can linger for a surprising length of time even after you've ceased to use them.

Chemical mood-changers of any kind can be a serious obstacle—often unrecognized or denied—to freeing yourself from debt. They can also become a problem in themselves.

20

SPECIALTIES

The following practices are sophisticated. They are not to everyone's taste, but many people have used them to powerful effect. They are offered here as options.

The Vacuum Principle

The Vacuum Principle is an extension of the concept of letting go, of releasing your grip upon something, of ceasing to cling to it, of allowing it to leave your life. It is more aggressive than simply letting go. In practicing it, you create a vacuum, an empty space in your life, by deliberately divesting yourself of something that is old, unwanted, or inferior. You do this in order to make room for something new and more desirable to enter. You do it even when—*particularly* when—you fear that you might not be able to replace it.

Anyone's life can become so cluttered that there is no room in it for anything new. When you're in trouble with debt, a fair amount of what fills your life—from clothes to kitchen equipment to furniture—can have become worn out, flawed, and second-rate. You may not be aware of this; you may have only a vague sense of tawdriness or insufficiency. Or if you are aware of it, you may think there's nothing you can do because you lack the money to replace something, or you tell yourself it's still serviceable, that you can make do with it. The result is blockage. Everything stays the same.

When you practice the Vacuum Principle, you evaluate what you have, which might be anything from an old tie to a television set. You ask: Do I really need this? Do I enjoy and take pleasure from it? If the answer is no, get rid of it: Give it away, sell it, or throw it out. Do so consciously, deliberately, in the faith and confidence that you are creating an empty space in your life into which, even if you can not imagine how at the moment, will flow the new, the more desirable, and the more pleasing.

Early in my recovery, I was aware for several months that I was dissatisfied with my sheets. One set was perfectly fine, but of a dark color that no longer suited my mood and had in fact begun to depress me. The rest were old, washed out, or frayed. I had little money to allocate to household furnishings then. But I decided to act anyway, to create a vacuum. Otherwise, nothing would change, I'd just keep living with what I had. I gave away the set that no longer suited me, kept just one—which I would have to strip from the bed each week, wash, and put back on the same night—and threw the rest out. Six weeks later I owned three new sets, which were of pleasing design and excellent quality, and my pleasure in life took a commensurate upward tick. Did some minor miraculous event occur? No. Once I'd created the vacuum, I was able to find the money in my Spending Plan, where I hadn't before.

Elizabeth, a secretary whose Spending Plan included only $50 a month for clothes, purged her apartment of every article that didn't make her feel wonderful to wear or that she didn't absolutely need. She had an accumulation of nearly fifteen years, going back to high school. Most of it went out. This was a courageous act. She needed the company of a friend when she did it, to keep her fear at bay. Fourteen months later, she now has a new wardrobe that is more than sufficient to cover all her needs, and she enjoys every piece in it, feels good about herself whenever she dresses.

The Vacuum Principle is applicable to situations as well as objects. Jack, who had training and experience as a video technician, had been driving a cab for three years, was unhappy with the work, and wasn't making the money he wanted. He'd been looking for an alternative in a desultory fashion for a year without result. He decided to create a vacuum by quitting the cab company, despite his fear that he would only eat up his contingency fund and then find himself out of money as well as work. He filled the vacuum he created with concentrated job hunting, and six weeks later was hired by a video corporation to do work he liked, at $24,000 more per year than he had been making.

That's the way it is with the Vacuum Principle. If you choose to work with it, it's best to begin on a small scale. You might, for example, want to go through your shirts or sweaters, culling out and divesting yourself of all but those that you truly like and enjoy or truly need. As you gain confidence that you are not going to end up living in lack, that the new and more pleasing will indeed enter the empty space you have created, you can begin to practice this principle on increasing levels of significance.

In and Out in 24 Hours

This is a demanding practice for most, especially the self-employed. It's not for everyone. It can make your hands sweat, your stomach go queasy:

You permit no bill to sit on your desk for more than twenty-four hours. Even if you have only $75 left and a bill for $60 arrives, you pay it immediately. You pay it knowing that you will generate whatever money you need and that you'll do so without debting. It comes in, it goes out: one day, twenty-four hours.

I first began this practice a year and a half into my recovery, in 1986. It was the sixth of the month. I had $1,700 in my checking account, $1,300 in bills backed up, and another $1,500 worth coming in. The next money due me wouldn't arrive for five to nine weeks. My expenses then were $2,700 a month. That was an apparent shortfall of anywhere from $1,100 to $3,800 over the coming two months. Apprehensive, I met with two people who work this program to discuss the situation.

At the time, I didn't have a dining table. I usually ate in the kitchen at a narrow counter, had to jury-rig something when my son was visiting, and was reluctant to have dinner company. I had priced tables and knew that a gateleg model, ideal for my circumstances, was then on sale for $200.

After reviewing the situation with me, Paul, one of the people with whom I met, said, "Tomorrow morning, go buy the table. Then sit down and pay every bill on your desk."

Mary, the other person, agreed.

"That'll leave me with $200," I said. "I don't know when I'll get the next money. It could be two months."

"You'll be all right," Paul said.

The next morning, I bought the table. That afternoon I paid the bills. My fear was overwhelming. Even my body didn't want to do it—I made mistakes on five of the six checks and had to write them over, and when I left the apartment I forgot the envelopes and had to go back for them. Depositing them in the mailbox, I felt as if the ground had fallen away beneath me.

So why did I do it, if it was such a powerful source of agitation? I did it in order to go forward in the face of my own fear, as an act of commitment, to strengthen myself—as a statement of faith in my own recovery, in my ability to generate all the money I needed to improve the quality of my life and meet my responsibilities without debting. Occasionally, working this program, some people take an action strictly on faith, which cannot be explicated convincingly to someone still intimidated by his own fear or inexperienced with these principles.

Seven weeks passed before the money that was due me did in fact reach me, but I didn't lack during that period. Other, unexpected money came in—consultancy work, a quick magazine assignment, dividends on an insurance policy, a small royalty check from a German edition of one of my novels that I didn't even know was still in print. I was all right, as Paul had said I would be.

Since then, I have paid my rent on the first of each month and for many years about 90 percent of all the bills I received within a 24-hour period. What about the other 10 percent? Sometimes my fear rose up, and I delayed for a couple of days, even a week or two, thinking, "This time it's not going to work. This time I'll go down in flames if I don't hang on to something." But that never happened, and wasn't likely to, so long as I kept working the program. These days, I simplify by writing out checks once a week, or more accurately, ordering them sent out, since I do most of my banking online. Each Saturday, I pay every bill in the house. It's one of the ways I don't debt, one day at a time.

In candor, "In and Out in 24 Hours" is a hard practice, and only a minority can bring themselves to do it. And I do not recommend that you try it outside the context of the entire program, without a solid body of recovery behind you, without the experience, belief, and confidence necessary to back yourself up. But if those conditions are met, it can be a powerful and valuable practice.

The Ideal Spending Plan

Get a blank copy of your Spending Plan. Pour a cup of coffee, sit down, and get comfortable.

Look at the first category. Think about it awhile. Disregarding wild flights of fancy—"I want a hundred-room castle or fifty sports cars"—consider: What would you like to be able to spend each month in this category? What do you think would make you feel reasonably comfortable and happy? Write that figure down in the vertical "Plan" column across from the category.

Now go to the next one. Reflect on it. How much would you like to be able to spend here? Write that figure down in the "Plan" column. Continue down your list of categories, one at a time. Enter an ideal figure—one you think would make you comfortable and happy—for each one.

When you're finished, pause for a few moments, stretch, and relax. Now look at that Spending Plan. This is a picture of what, at this moment, would be an ideal life for you. It doesn't really seem all that outrageous, does it? It's not. If you use the techniques and concepts of this book on a daily basis, you have an excellent chance of moving yourself right into your Ideal Spending Plan, and beyond it.

What, Precisely, Do You Want?

One of the biggest impediments to getting what you want in life is not knowing what that is. It's hard to plan a trip when you don't know where you wish to go. You need a clear idea of your destination before you have any reasonable hope of arriving there.

The Ideal Spending Plan is a good start—it provides you with a sense of how you'd like to be living, at least as far as today is concerned. But it's only a start. The following is a discovery process that will help you become more specific, that will reveal to you what you truly want in your life.

Sit down with a pen and a pad of paper. Across the top of

the page write, *If I could be, do, and have everything I want:*
Beneath it, list the following categories.

Work/Career
Money
Lifestyle/Possessions
Relationships
Creative Self-Expression
Leisure Activities
Personal Growth/Education

Make each category a heading, and under each heading
write out a paragraph or two that would describe your ideal
scene—if you could be and do and have everything you
want. Let go of all your inhibitions when you do this, of all
sense of restriction and limitation, anything that says to
you, "I can't have, I can't be, I can't do." Unleash your
wishes and desires. Let them run free. Write your descrip-
tions in the present tense, as if you are already there. For
example:

"I'm living in the country in a large white frame house
that's flooded with morning light. There's a rolling lawn,
large oak trees, a flower garden . . .

"I'm earning $125,000 a year. I've been out of debt for a
long time. I have an investment portfolio worth $400,000. It
pays me an additional $50,000 a year in dividends. I buy
presents for my friends and family . . .

"I work only four days a week. I play tennis every weekend. I fly to the Caribbean to go scuba diving. I spend time
in galleries, and enjoy doing fine woodworking . . ."

When you're done, read over what you've written. This is
a clear picture of how you would really like to live, what you
want, what is meaningful to you, and what would please
you. It is quite valuable. Having a sense of this—your ideal
state—in mind will help guide you as you make decisions

and undertake beneficial actions, and will keep you aimed in directions you truly wish to go.

Another approach is to make a "List of 100." Again, be as fanciful as you wish, but list only things that you would *truly* like to be, do, or have, not things that you think you *ought* to.

The lists might look something like this:

100 THINGS I WOULD LIKE TO BE

1. A pilot
2. Fluent in Italian
3. A swimmer
4. Well read
5. An Egyptologist
6. A chef
7. A skilled dancer
8. A passenger on a flight to Mars
9. The life of the party
10. A talk-show host . . .

100 THINGS I WOULD LIKE TO DO

1. Get up early in the morning
2. Go fishing every week
3. Climb Mt. Washington
4. Study history
5. Date only terrific people
6. Build my own house
7. Live in a warm climate
8. Sky-dive
9. Go to Greece
10. Raise dogs . . .

100 THINGS I WOULD LIKE TO HAVE

1. A summer cabin on a lake
2. One copy of every edition of *Moby Dick* ever published
3. A great sound system

4. A BMW convertible
5. A pair of oxblood dress shoes
6. A flat-screen monitor
7. A blue silk tie
8. An emotionally stable lover
9. A two-bedroom condominium
10. $150,000 in liquid assets . . .

Some people have trouble with this, fearing they'll only feel worse if they point out to themselves all the things they'd like to have that they don't have. But that's a spurious fear. Your subconscious *already knows* what you want—you've just been hiding it from yourself, that's all. Which only undermines your chances of ever getting it; the fear of not being able to have it ends up fulfilling itself.

Linda, a medical technician, had been so beaten down by her debts that she couldn't permit herself even to *conceive* of an ideal scene or make more than a few entries on her lists. The continual stress and despair of her debts had destroyed her capacity to imagine any other kind of life. She worked this program four months before she was able to write the lists out. Within six months after that, she had achieved several of the things she had written down, including a change of employers and a new apartment.

An impressive number of your entries will appear in your life in short order, once you clarify to yourself what it is that you really want.

If you have trouble writing out the lists or scenes at first, just keep at them. Try them every two weeks. As your subconscious realizes that you're taking increasing control of your life and that there's no reason to fear, it will begin to open up.

The more fun you have with the process, the more benefit you'll get from it. It's not supposed to be work. The purpose is simply to reveal to yourself what you'd truly like out of life and to help you break free of the restrictions in your own thinking. And remember that your wants are not carved in granite. You're not committed to them simply because you've written them down. They will change as you change, and with time. It's good to draw up a new set once or twice a year. It helps you stay abreast of and knowledgeable about your own changing desires. Each time you do, take a look at the old ones. You'll be surprised to discover how many of the things you wanted you've already brought into your life, and how you've begun to move in the direction of your ideal scenes.

Targeting

It's much easier to accomplish goals and effect change when you have a clear vision of what you're after. Targeting is a good way to refine that vision.

Read over your ideal scenes. Fix them in your mind and keep them there while you go through the following process. In the end, your goals—no matter how small or apparently removed the immediate ones are—should all contribute in some way toward helping you realize your ideal scenes. Sit down with your pad of paper. Across the top, write:

Five-Year Goals

In terms of moving you toward your ideal scenes, list ten goals you would like to accomplish by five years from now. Be reasonable, but don't think small. Five years is a good chunk of time. To illustrate, let's say your goals are these:

1. Be free of debt.
2. Live in a house in the country.
3. Be married.
4. Speak Italian.
5. Climb Mt. Washington.

6. Raise dogs.

7. Have a $100,000 investment portfolio.

8. Be a talk-show host.

9. Do fine woodworking as a hobby.

10. Own an extensive and elegant wardrobe.

Now write:

One-Year Goals

Under this heading, draw up a list of seven goals for the coming year that would contribute toward helping you realize your five-year goals. Make them goals you think you have a reasonably good chance of accomplishing over the next year. Working from the previous list, these could be:

1. Be well under way with a Repayment Plan.

2. Finish one semester of a beginner's course in Italian.

3. Know just *where* in the country I think I'd like to live.

4. Be familiar with the range of possibilities for being a talk-show host, from local radio to network television.

5. Make my first investment or investments, regardless of the amount involved.

6. Be meeting people who are more suitable to marriage than not.

7. Own half a dozen excellent and beautiful articles of clothing.

When you're finished write:

One-Month Goals

Here, list five goals you'd like to achieve in the next thirty days that would act in support of your one-year goals. Based upon our listed one-year goals, these might be:

1. Make a list of my creditors and figure out what percentage of my total debt represents the amount I owe each.
2. Learn the names of half a dozen individuals or schools that offer courses in Italian.
3. Know roughly how many talk shows are available on television and radio in my area and what they're like.
4. Meet someone new who might be pleasant to go out with.
5. Know what the price range is for the first piece of clothing I'm going to buy for my new wardrobe.

When you've done this, write:

One-Week Goals

Under this heading, list five goals you'd like to accomplish in the coming week that would help you to realize your goals for the month. Based on our listed thirty-day goals, this could be:

1. Create a Spending Plan.
2. Ask three friends who might know people and places offering courses in Italian.
3. Check one day's radio listing, marking with a highlight pen all the talk shows offered.
4. List the five qualities that would be most important to me in a spouse.
5. Decide what *kind* of article of clothing is probably the most reasonable for me to purchase as the first piece in my new wardrobe—for instance, a blouse, tie, scarf, or pair of shoes.

As you'll note from the examples, the larger the time frame involved, the larger a goal will be; conversely, the smaller the time frame, the smaller the goal. One of your goals for five years from now, for example, is to be debt-free—but your goal for the coming week, in the service of that larger goal, is simply to create a Spending Plan. Another five-year goal is to possess an extensive and elegant wardrobe—yet for this week your goal is nothing more than to *decide* what single article of new clothing would be most pleasing and possible for you to buy first.

You begin with a definite vision of what you eventually want on the large scale, and then reduce it downward into ever smaller actions or goals as you approach nearer to today. This ensures that all of your actions, no matter how small, move you closer to your goals for the week or month, and in turn those will advance you steadily toward your large-scale goals, which are much further off.

A final point about goals is they are *not* something you *have* to achieve. A goal should not be a lash on your back nor a mechanism of potential failure. Rather, it should be a sign-post to help keep you on track. Of the five goals you set for any given week, you'll probably accomplish only two to four; you may want to carry an unrealized goal over into the following week, or you may want to abandon it in favor of a new one.

Your goals will change as new ideas occur to you, new desires. That's fine. Rethinking or redefining them is a legitimate part of targeting. Have fun with the process. Keep it simple and enjoy it.

The Real Stuff

Nothing makes money more real than going on a hard-cash basis to the fullest extent possible. This is not the same as simply not debting. This is keeping your check-writing and use of your debit card, prepaid phone card, and other prepaid cards and vouchers to an absolute minimum—only what is most easily paid through the mail, such as rent and utility bills—and paying for everything else in cash, in real dollars and cents.

If you do this—if you handle the actual fives, tens, twenties, fifties, and hundreds, paying real currency in as many transactions as you can—you will rapidly gain a vivid sense of the significance, use, management, power, and enjoyment of money. Most people who do this also find it provides them with a sense of freedom and of true entitlement to their money.

Generosity

Generosity is a quality of unselfishness, *not* self-sacrifice. It is a regard for the well-being and happiness of another. It is important not only in giving, but in receiving. Difficulty in either giving or receiving restricts the flow of money into your life, retards the process of liberation from debt, and inhibits prosperity.

Those who can't give easily generally don't believe they have enough for themselves. Those who can't receive easily often see themselves as unworthy, or confuse receiving with charity, or think of it as less virtuous than giving, or are afraid they'll be expected to give something back in return.

Giving Anyone can afford to give, no matter what his condition. It is only the belief that you are unable to that prevents you. If you don't have $1,000 to give, you have $100. If you don't have $100, then $50. If not $50, then $20. If not $20, $10. If not $10, $5. If not $5, then a dollar, and if not a dollar, then a dime. Or you can give time, listening to a friend who needs to talk, volunteering it to a church, a recycling center, any other place whose work appeals to you. You can use your talents to make gifts: instruction, a drawing, a loaf of baked bread. You can give your affection by reaching out through phone calls and letters.

To give means to make a present of, to bestow. And you can do that.

Why should you? Nothing says that you should. But developing a capacity to give helps demolish the distorted belief that you don't have anything, that there's so little for you that you can't afford to give any of it away. It mitigates the anger that springs from the old belief that life or others are somehow responsible for your situation and that you're helpless to correct it. It helps you begin to see your own abundance.

The more you give—freely and without resentment, for the sheer sake of giving—the more you receive. What you radiate outward is what you attract back to yourself.

Receiving In the eyes of the universe, or whatever else there may be, you are as worthy as any other human being. You may not fully believe that yet, but by now you ought to recognize that any residual doubts you have on the question stem strictly from old, distorted perceptions of yourself. You are as deserving and entitled to receive as any other person on this planet.

There are people who feel there's something inherently wrong with receiving—for *them;* often they're the first to raise their voice on behalf of everyone else's right to receive. They believe their own predestined role is to do without, or that there is some kind of merit in not receiving, or that they are too "strong" to "need" to receive, or they mistake their own pleasure in it or yearning for it as greed, as weakness, and therefore something to be crushed and denied.

If someone compliments your dress, do you respond with something like "Oh, this old thing. It was nice once, but it's wearing out now," or "I got it on sale"? If you're told you're a handsome man, do you say, "Well, thanks, I guess this light makes me look good," or "You should see my brother; he's really a good-looking guy"? When someone gives you a present, do you say, "You shouldn't have," or "It's lovely, but really, it's too much," or "Thanks, but you didn't have to," or even "I wish you hadn't"?

These may seem insignificant at first, but they reveal a reluctance to receive, even on a small level. This reluctance grows more powerful as it advances up the chain, and at the top it can effectively prevent you from accepting your own abundance.

A good discipline is to begin to practice receiving—when you're given anything at all, from a compliment to money—as graciously as you can, to refrain from saying anything more than "Thank you." This requires strength and discipline of some people at first. They want mightily to deflect the gift, to disqualify, reduce, or humble themselves in some way. The harder it is for you to say simply "Thank you" and then stop, to say nothing more, the clearer it should be to you that you *need* to learn to receive.

Early on, still reeling from the effects of my former debting, I had to face Christmas, and this hard and painful fact: No matter how I contorted my Spending Plan, I had no money for presents. None. This verged on torment. Most of my life, I had spent a great deal on Christmas presents, especially for my two children; it was something I wanted to do, that I enjoyed doing, that gave me a lot of pleasure.

What I did that Christmas—though it wasn't easy; in fact, damn difficult—was inform the people I customarily bought gifts for, including my two sons, that while I regretted it and loved them and would be thinking of them, I had no money for gifts this year.

My youngest son was fourteen then. He was with me for the weekend. He listened with a seriousness that was caused by my own discomfort.

He said, "That's okay, Dad. I understand. You shouldn't feel bad." Then he brightened, and with excitement said, "I already know what I'm getting you. I think you're going to like it a lot."

Instantly I said, "Don't get me anything, Jesse. I don't want a present."

His face changed. His excitement vanished, the joy died. He looked like he'd been kicked in the stomach, like I'd whipped him. I felt sick. We were both silent.

What I did next was hard—because I didn't want anything from him, because I couldn't *accept* anything from him, since I was failing him and didn't deserve anything—but I forced myself to apologize, to say that I understood, that it was fine, that he *could* give me a present and that I'd be happy to get it.

His eyes grew moist—they don't often do that—and he hugged me, and in a few moments he was his usual cheerful self again.

What I had done, because of my own inability to receive, was to rip away from my son his right to give me a gift, to do something for me that he wanted to do. I turned him away, rejected him; I had hurt him at that moment, and badly. That's what an inability to receive can do to others around you.

I did give gifts to my sons that Christmas. I gave them what I could. I wrote them each a very personal letter, speaking of their lives, from my first moments with them onward, and telling them how much they had meant to me, how much they did mean to me now, and how much I loved them.

I gave something else to them that Christmas too, and gave the same thing to myself and everyone else I know, though it is an abstract thing and more difficult to grasp, and I could not see it then. I gave them my own recovery. I gave them a father, a son, a brother, lover, friend, fellow-traveler, and acquaintance who had brought the downward spiral to an end and who was growing stronger, healthier, clearer, and more capable every day—perhaps more than he had ever been, even in the years before the trouble with debt began.

There is a great stream that is at once both giving and receiving. The inability to practice either cuts off the flow of that stream, and without it life is drier, less hospitable and satisfying, and prosperity and plenitude have a harder time taking root.

21

IT'S A
BIG UNIVERSE

This chapter is brief. It is brief because it is about spirituality, and that is a personal subject; yet it is a subject relevant to everyone, regardless of how one feels about religion.

Spirituality is not synonymous with religion. It requires neither creed nor code, nor even belief in the existence of any kind of god. Atheists and agnostics can be as spiritual as priests and rabbis. Spirituality is simply an awareness that you are not the center of the universe; it is an intuitive sense of a vital principle or animating force. It is an overview, a broader perspective, the apprehension that there is something "more." It is a yearning, a perception, a movement toward connection with that force or principle.

Traditional Chinese paintings depict vast landscapes—towering mountains, plummeting valleys—and in one part, tiny figures that are people. That is the perspective we're talking about, the same perspective that steals upon us when we sit by the side of an ocean or look up into the star-filled immensity of the night sky.

However You Understand It

What is, or whatever may be, the context in which we live, has been called by many names. Among them are:

- The Infinite
- The Source
- The Unknowable
- God
- Energy
- The Uncaused Cause
- Spirit
- Being
- Higher Self
- The Universe
- Divine Thought
- The Ultimate
- Infinite Love
- Grace
- Prime Mover
- Presence
- The Absolute
- Creation
- Universal Flow
- Radiance
- Higher Power

The name is not important. Whatever it may or may not be, it's large enough to wear comfortably any costume we might wish to throw over it. However we understand it is fine.

Spirituality, connection with what you understand the life force to be, is a powerful agent of centering, of peace and serenity, and of effecting internal change. Developing it is basically a process of letting go of self-will. That doesn't mean abdicating responsibility, failing to plan, or ceasing to take action. It means recognizing and admitting that you don't have all the answers, that your old ways, attitudes, and perceptions didn't work, that you are not God, that you are not the center of the universe. It is a willingness to trust what is best in yourself, to become still, to become open and receptive to inner guidance, to let go of fear and despair, and to know that at any given moment you are perfectly all right and as integral a part of the universe as any other human being.

There are many ways to cultivate spirituality—everything from quiet walks through the countryside to meditation and formal prayer. How you do it is less important than *that* you do it. Spirituality is a tremendous resource, a deep well of strength and comfort.

Be still, and open yourself to what is.

22

Staying Out: Part 1

It's nice to be debt-free, or on your way to freedom. Remember how it was when you couldn't think about anything else, how it sucked the color out of your life and poisoned your days? You don't want to go back. You don't want to forget how you got there, how it felt, and start the whole sad story over again. You want to stay out of debt. Here's how you do it.

The Three Cardinal Rules

1. Don't debt, one day at a time.
2. Keep the Spending Record scrupulously.
3. Adhere closely to your Spending Plan.

If you do nothing else at all, do this. It may seem ridiculously self-evident, but you simply *can not* go back into debt if you follow these three simple rules.

Nothing Can Make You Debt

Nothing can make you debt. Remember that. No one's going to put a gun to your head and threaten to blow your brains out unless you borrow money from him. You may want to debt—with every cell in your body—but nothing can *make* you do it.

There is always another way to meet your needs. Rethink the situation. Find that way.

You never have to debt again.

Use This Book

Back to the Black is a living program, not a theory. It works to the degree that you are willing to work it. This book won't do you much good if it's gathering dust on a shelf. Use it. Work with it. Integrate its material into your life on a daily basis. The more you do, the better off you'll be. If you practice its techniques and absorb its concepts, you *will* liberate yourself from debt, you *will* stay free, and you *will* go on to live in prosperity and abundance.

Fool Me Once, Shame on You; Fool Me Twice, Shame on Me

There is enormous advertising pressure to borrow money, use credit, and spend more. We live in a virtual sea of it but are rarely aware of it on a conscious level.

James, a photographer, liquidated $19,000 worth of debt over four years. Gradually he drifted away from the regimens of this program, wasn't seen by his support group for several months, then suddenly reappeared, with $6,500 in new debt.

"What happened?" someone asked.

James shrugged ruefully. "I was surrounded by insurmountable opportunities," he said.

The more conscious you become of this advertising pressure to debt—the more you see it for what it is—the easier it will be to resist. Sensitize yourself to the number of times you are invited, urged, and prompted to use credit every day.

Make a game of it. At intervals, keep score for a day or a week on a piece of paper. Listen to the radio ads, the television ads. Look at the ads in your newspaper, in magazines. Note the solicitations you receive in the mail, the pamphlets in your bank, the credit card fliers next to cash registers, the posters and tear-offs in public transportation.

- "Fly now, pay later."
- "Take advantage of new low interest rates."
- "Only twelve low monthly payments."
- "Your preapproved credit line."
- "Accepted everywhere."
- "Time-option payment plan."
- "Just sign and return this agreement today."
- "Call our toll-free operator."
- "Send no money now."
- "No membership fee."

This can be a revelation. With scarcely any effort—nothing but heightened awareness—you'll find that you can score ten, twenty, or more on a given day. Not only has the door to debt been thrown wide open for you, but there's someone waving you through at every moment: Pick a debt, any debt.

Thank you, but no. I've already had the experience.

How Could Anyone Do That (Now That I'm Not)?

Build a sensitivity toward signs and reports of debting problems among your friends and associates and people in the news.

Once a month or so, keep score for a couple of days. Spot

friends going on mood-changing shopping sprees. Listen to people complain about money, bills, a creditor. Note the number of credit cards they carry. Look for news stories and magazine articles on debt and credit and about people who embezzled from their companies, abused political office, committed crimes, or even killed themselves because of debt.

Once you've sensitized yourself to them, you'll find that there are legions upon legions who are plunging deeper into debt every day. You can scarcely get through a day without running into them, seeing them, or hearing or reading about them several times. This awareness will help you remember how far you've come, how it was for you back then, and just why you want to remain debt-free.

Those Good Friends

Your support group is a valuable tool. Don't drift away from it once you're out of debt or on your way out. Continue your involvement with it. Maintain contact with the people in it by telephone. This will strengthen your purpose, keep your vision clear, offer you ever increasing options and alternatives, and help you to move forward into a larger and more pleasing way of life.

23

STAYING OUT:
PART 2

The following principles are true for everyone who works the Back to the Black program. But they're largely a matter of discernment. Like optical illusions, you won't see them until you begin to search for them. They're there. All you have to do is look.

The Money Comes In

When you're committed not to incur new debt and you practice the principles of this program, there is always enough; the money comes in.

How?

I don't know, precisely, and I don't think anyone else does either. It has to do with the combined impact of each of the various parts of the program. But I've seen it again and again in my own life and in the lives of others. If the commitment not to incur new debt is *unconditional*, and if the program is worked, the money comes in.

That doesn't mean that you always get what you want, or

when you want it, or in the form you want it. There are set-backs, there are what appear to be major defeats, there are painful moments. But in the end, the money comes in. Sometimes in agonizingly slow dribbles, sometimes in spuming cascades. Sometimes mundanely, sometimes in a flamboyant event.

Cheryl, a landscape designer, eked by one day at a time for a year and a half, never knowing in any given month just how she was going to meet next month's expenses. Then over the next two years her reputation spread, she gained repeat business, old clients recommended her to new clients, she was written up in a regional magazine; now she has to employ subcontractors.

Bob, a musician and comedian who'd made a lot of money when he was quite young and had then slipped into obscurity for more than a decade, worked small gigs, did private coaching, and took an occasional office temporary job for nearly three years. He's now in a comeback, making more than $175,000 a year.

Max, a technical writer who was early in recovery and still stabilizing, called his insurance broker to say that he couldn't pay his life insurance premium, he had to cancel the policy. His broker informed him that $950 in dividends had accumulated. Max used $350 to pay the premium and had his broker send him a check for the $600 balance.

Marie, an administrative assistant, was fired from her $40,000-a-year job and was out of work for three months. She exhausted her contingency fund, got down to her last $12, which she spent on dinner at a Chinese restaurant with a friend, and was hired the next day at $56,000 a year.

The variations are infinite. Why it works is open to debate; *that* it works is not. I've never seen anyone with a total commitment not to debt, have to debt.

The money comes in. There is always enough.

Commonplace Miracles

A commitment not to debt shifts you—whether that was your intention or not—into a life of increasing options and alternatives, where as time passes and you gain experience you begin to understand that there are very few limits except those you impose upon yourself.

As you take positive action, positive results appear, frequently in unexpected ways and often continuing to reverberate over an extended period—sometimes long after the original action has been forgotten, and in a fashion wholly unimagined at the time.

As you replace old and distorted beliefs with new and healthy ones, clarity increases, emotions lift. As you assume control of your life, the fear begins to recede. As you emerge from debt, the pain falls away. As you become self-reliant, your sense of well-being burgeons.

All these, the events and quality of your life, the influxes of money, are miracles in the original sense of the word—wondrous happenings—and they do indeed become commonplace.

Opportunity Knocked and I Wasn't Home

Opportunity doesn't knock once. It's pounding on the door, tearing off the roof, and kicking in the windows all the time. It's a matter of perspective, of being willing and ready to see it.

Andrew and Nan, two friends both involved with debt recovery, were having dinner with a mutual friend who was unaware of their situation but who knew both were unhappy in their current jobs. He mentioned an opening in the marketing department of a company he did business with. Andrew scarcely listened because he had no experience in marketing. Neither did Nan but she called anyway, found that they were willing to train, and went for an interview. She liked the company and the work. They liked her. She started as a research analyst at $10,000 a year more than she had been making.

Erica is fast-witted and funny. She keeps her friends in stitches. So's Mike. He keeps his friends in stitches too. He also makes an extra $5,500 a year selling material freelance to a publisher of joke greeting cards.

Opportunity runs through our lives like colors through a rainbow. Seeing it is a matter of perspective, of being willing and ready.

Where Is It Written That You Have to Work for Money?

"Work" is usually perceived as necessary drudgery: People work like a dog, they gotta make a living, they slave at the office. But with few exceptions, the most successful people are those who do what they most enjoy or what's most meaningful to them. They don't "work"—not in the sense of unpleasant toil or strain, waiting for the day to be over. What they do is engage in an activity they find significant or that gives them pleasure. It may be difficult, it may require effort or long hours, but that's beside the point—because they're doing what they *want* to do, not what they think they ought to or have to.

If you hate your job or are bored with it, you're not likely to make much money at it in the long run, regardless of how potentially well paying it is. Sooner or later you'll mess it up in some way or resign yourself to simply going through the motions, wondering now and then, with some wistfulness, why life turned out to be so gray, flat, and disappointing.

Even if what excites you seems to offer little possibility of making reasonable money, in most cases you're still better off doing it—you'll find a way to get what you truly need from it, and a large part of what you want.

Most of my professors, and practically everyone else, discouraged me from even *thinking* of becoming a professional writer. It was nice to write, I was told, but I had to think of what I was going to do for a living—advertising maybe, public relations, teaching. But I didn't want to do advertising, or public relations, or teach; I wanted to write, despite the apparent impossibility of that. (Today, the average freelance writer makes less than $8,000 a year; then, the figure was even smaller.) I held two jobs after I graduated—the first for three months; the second, nine. Then, for the next thirty-odd years, I wrote (with a brief period as an editor).

I did and still do what I most enjoy and what's most meaningful to me. I found ways to get what I truly needed from it, and a large part of what I wanted.

With few exceptions, the people who are the most successful and happiest in their lives also do what they most enjoy and what is most meaningful to them—whether that involves flying commercial airliners from coast to coast or fixing outboard motors in the north woods.

Prosperity & Abundance

We've used these words—prosperity and abundance—frequently in this book. They are, in the end, the true goal and purpose of this program. For some people they conjure up images of big money, expensive cars, luxury apartments. That's fine, if that's what you want. But prosperity and abundance don't necessarily have anything to do with dollars and cents.

Prosperity is a condition of thriving, of steady improvement.

Abundance is a plentiful supply, more than sufficient.

Both are states of being that describe the quality of a life, not numbers on a ledger sheet. Money is definitely a part of that—and I don't know anyone working this program who isn't interested in some kind of increase in money—but it is only a part. The rest has to do with the way in which you live your life, how it feels to you on a daily basis.

The truth is that coming to live with a present sense of real prosperity and abundance is what brings in the money, rather than the other way around.

This program is an inside job.

24

SUPPLEMENTARY MATTERS

Debtors Anonymous

There is no better or more effective support group for anyone with a debt problem. To obtain a meeting list or help in forming a chapter in your area, get in touch with DA by email or postal mail at:

da-gso@mindspring.com

Or...

Debtors Anonymous, General Service Office
P.O. Box 920888
Needham, MA 02492-0009
Telephone: 781-453-2743
http://www.debtorsanonymous.org

Inquiries are kept strictly confidential. While all inquiries will be answered, DA encourages correspondents to use email for the quickest response.

Books

Most large bookstores contain sections on personal finance which offer many general and specialized books. Books on other subjects can also be used to good advantage. Here are a few titles of special usefulness:

Bolles, Richard Nelson. *What Color Is Your Parachute?* Berkeley, CA: Ten Speed Press, 2002. (Updated every year.) A practical manual for job-hunters and career-changers. This book has been *the* definitive work on the subject for more than twenty-five years. The exercises take time and thought, but are worth the effort.

Burns, David D., M.D. *Feeling Good: The New Mood Therapy*. New York: William Morrow, 1980. A readable exposition of cognitive psychology, which concerns itself with dysfunctional attitudes and perceptions that result in self-crippling depression and anxiety. Offers effective techniques for reworking these into realistic and beneficial ones.

Clason, George S. *The Richest Man in Babylon*. New York: Hawthorn Books, 1955. A slim volume on personal finance presented in the style of parables. Clear, comprehensive treatment of basic principles.

de Mello, Anthony. *One Minute Wisdom*. New York: Image Books, 1985. Unfortunate title; excellent anthology. Small parable/lessons drawn from the mystical traditions of East and West. The Master in these little tales is not one but many: a Hindu guru, a Zen roshi, a Taoist sage, a Jewish rabbi, a Christian monk, and a Sufi mystic. Anything by de Mello, an East Indian Jesuit and spiritual director, is worth reading.

Dolan, Ken and Daria. *Smart Money: How to Be Your Own Financial Manager*. New York: Berkley Books, 1990. Personal banking, home-buying, insurance, mutual funds, taxes, retirement plans, and similar topics. Each covered in a single chapter presented in the form of common questions with short, simple answers. Slightly dated but still a good and useful general reference work.

Leonard, Robin and Deanne Loonin. *Money Troubles: Legal Strategies to Cope with Your Debts,* 7th edition. Berkeley, CA: Nolo Press, 2001. Legal strategies for coping with debts of various kinds, from student loans to alimony. Leonard and Loonin are attorneys. Very helpful short-term, nuts-and-bolts material.

LeShan, Lawrence. *How to Meditate.* Boston and Toronto: Little, Brown & Co., 1974. Reprint, Boston and Toronto: Back Bay Books, 1999. A simple yet comprehensive work explaining the nature of meditation, its psychological and physical benefits, and various ways to go about it. A pioneering work when first published, this slim volume remains one of the best introductions to meditation available.

Mundis, Jerrold. *Earn What You Deserve: How to Stop Underearning & Start Thriving.* New York: Bantam Books, 1995. To underearn is repeatedly to make less money than you need on which to live humanely, despite your desire and best efforts to do otherwise. This book shows step-by-step how to reverse that and transform money from a source of anxiety into something that enhances life.

Mundis, Jerrold. *Making Peace with Money.* Kansas City, MO: Andrews McMeel, 1999. A comprehensive program for creating a relationship with money that is free of stress, worry, or pain; one that is satisfying, even joyful. Each chapter addresses a different aspect of money, such as debt, spending, work, generosity, vision, and wealth; provides practical techniques to bring about positive change in those areas; and includes quotes, tales, and parables meant to illuminate them from such diverse sources as the Bible, Zen Buddhism, Sufi teaching stories, the Talmud, folklore, mythology, and both ancient and contemporary philosophy.

Schor, Juliet B. *The Overspent American: Upscaling, Down-shifting, and the New Consumer.* New York: Basic Books, 1998. A significant book. Schor, a leisure economist and university professor, analyzes the crisis that has overtaken middle-class and upper-middle-class America—a culture in which spending has become the ultimate social act. Her conclusions are original and compelling, including the concepts of competitive spending and community referent groups (in which members' varying incomes cause constant pressure on lower-end earners to escalate their spending upward toward that of higher-end earners), with the lives of television-series characters becoming absorbed into the referent community. Valuable in helping the reader rethink spending and bring about personal change.

Tobias, Andrew. *The Only Investment Guide You'll Ever Need*, 2002 Edition. New York: Harvest Books, 2002. The most recent revision of a very good book that comes close to living up to its title. Amusingly written and sound, most of it deals with clear, accessible, down-to-earth investment strategies, with some good comments on dealing with money in general to boot.

Magazines & Newspapers

Many general publications from *Esquire* to *Redbook* have columns on money and personal finance. Get in the habit of reading them. The more you know, the better equipped you are to deal with your money.

Most major newspapers have a financial or business section. It's helpful to skim these. They often contain articles on debt, credit, and spending.

Money magazine, *Consumer Reports, Kiplinger's Personal Finance,* and *Worth* are all useful.

If you own a business or are an investor, *Forbes* magazine, *The Wall Street Journal,* and *Barron's* are valuable aids.

Online Resources

There are numerous financial sites online, with vast amounts of information. If you have a focus, and exercise a little discipline, you can thread your way through them and find much that is useful. Without focus and discipline, though, you're likely to become quickly overwhelmed. Here are two sites where you might start:

http://www.smartmoney.com

http://www.bankrate.com

Another is the website for women, http://www.ivillage. com, at its section "Deep in Debt," which can be found under the general heading "Money." This section currently contains five message boards, including one for how-to questions about debt, another focused on compulsive spending, and another that functions as a support group. These boards have offered sound postings for several years. Males, while not made to feel unwelcome, are a marked minority here and often not seen at all. But there is no reason a male can't lurk and benefit from these postings even if he doesn't feel comfortable posting himself.

There are also Debtors Anonymous mailing lists online. These lists comprise members of the program who wish to communicate with one another across time and distance, members who live in areas where there are no meetings within easy driving distance, and people who think the program may be appropriate for them and want to determine if it is. Information on joining these lists can be found on DA's website at: http://www.debtorsanonymous.org.

Professional Advisers

It's foolish to try to save money by doing without professional help when there are important documents to sign, crises such as a threatened mortgage foreclosure, or large amounts of money at stake.

The most commonly used advisers are attorneys, accountants, financial planners, business managers, and professional agents. When you have a lot to gain or lose, they are nearly always worth more than the fee you'll pay them.

The best way to find a good professional is through personal referral—someone you know who's used him or her with good results. Lacking that, you can get referrals through professional societies such as your local Bar Association. The location and telephone numbers of the central offices of these societies can be found in your local library in the *Encyclopedia of Associations*.

Psychotherapy

I have seen few people bring their debting to a halt through psychotherapy alone. But I've seen many accomplish it with the Back to the Black program, even after failing with substantial therapy. Once the cycle of debting is broken—through action, by following the guidelines here—therapy can be a useful adjunct. When I first wrote this book, the helping professions were scarcely aware of what are now being called the money disorders—debting, hoarding, underearning, and compulsive spending. Fortunately, that is changing. More and more therapists are coming to recognize not only that these conditions exist, and that they are serious problems in their own right, but also that if left untreated they can inhibit and make more difficult and even impossible successful treatment of other, apparently unrelated conditions.

The best way to find a therapist, as with other kinds of professionals, is through personal referral by someone who's worked with that person to good effect. If you can't get a personal referral, call your local Mental Health Association and they will help you find a qualified practitioner.

Institutions, Organizations, & Corporations

Most city and county governments have a consumer affairs or consumer protection bureau. You can find them in your phone directory. Many corporations now offer credit and debt counseling to their employees through their employee assistance program or human resources division. Some unions and professional societies do too. There are courses in personal finance and money management available through community service organizations, university cooperative extension divisions, and adult education programs around the country. Any of these may be helpful.

A Closing Note

There is no reason for you to be in debt. You can free yourself from it entirely and remain free forever. You have already begun, by reading this book. If you integrate its concepts into your life and practice its techniques, one day at a time, you are bound to be successful.

I wish you a life of prosperity and abundance. . . .

About the Author

Jerrold Mundis is a writer, speaker, and counselor. His books have been selected by the Book-of-the-Month Club, Literary Guild, One Spirit Book Club, and others, and translated into a dozen foreign languages. His short work has appeared in such publications as the *New York Times Magazine* and *American Heritage*. A recovered debtor himself, he is intimately familiar with the success of the Debtors Anonymous program.

Jerry speaks regularly on debt and personal money for clients ranging from the U.S. Customs Service to the National Education Association, Unity Church, and professional societies and associations. He also works privately with individuals.

Jerry lives in New York City and can be reached at:

jerry@mundismoney.com